Brattleboro

Main Street, Brattleboro, Vermont, 1880s.

Brattleboro

HISTORICALLY SPEAKING

FRAN LYNGGAARD HANSEN

THE History PRESS

Published by The History Press
Charleston, SC 29403
www.historypress.net

First published 2009

Manufactured in the United States

ISBN 978.1.59629.719.7

Library of Congress Cataloging-in-Publication Data

Hansen, Fran Lynggaard.
Brattleboro : historically speaking / Fran Lynggaard Hansen.
p. cm.
Includes bibliographical references and index.
ISBN 978-1-59629-719-7 (alk. paper)
1. Brattleboro (Vt.)--History. 2. Brattleboro (Vt.)--Social life and customs. I. Title.
F59.B8H36 2009
974.3'9--dc22
2009017633

For Clarence and Cynthia Fairchild,
who encouraged in me a taste for all things historical.

CONTENTS

Preface

A WORD ABOUT THE ILLUSTRATIONS

The Brattleboro Historical Society has been quietly accumulating a fascinating and varied array of photographs and objects for years. Every week, people from across the nation and abroad call or write with questions specific to their families' local history, or to ask about an object they might own in their search for understanding of its meaning. The society is composed of volunteers who give hours and hours of their time in support of keeping our local history alive.

If you have pictures that could contribute to this historical collection, please consider allowing the society to scan your photographs. So many times people think that what they have to offer has little or no meaning or relevance, but the truth is that this is often not the case.

The majority of the art in this book is from the collection of the Brattleboro Historical Society, unless otherwise noted. Many of the pictures are actually postcards. Postcards hold a unique place in historical significance.

The oldest postcard printed here is from 1869. With the majority of townspeople without access to photography equipment at that time, it was common for local photographers and roaming businessmen to photograph disasters, such as the floods of 1927 and 1936, or to document new wonders of the modern age, such as the iron suspension bridges built across the Connecticut River. Local people purchased the cards to send to family and friends to allow them to witness the changes to their homes and communities.

Many years later, often local businesses did the same. Do you remember when the mom and pop hotels offered guests postcards of their establishments? How many children received a postcard of a motel with a big X on the door of the room Daddy stayed in last night on his travels for his job?

Postcard, late 1800s.

I am grateful for the assistance of the Brattleboro Historical Society and to all who were willing to share their photographs with me.

INTRODUCTION

In November 2004, when the Boston Red Sox won their first World Series in eighty-nine years, the *Brattleboro Reformer* was soliciting memories from local readers about their own personal histories with the Red Sox. I submitted an article and was called by the editor of the newspaper and asked if I would like to write a weekly column about life in Brattleboro. Thus the column "Downstreet" was born.

I envisioned "Downstreet" as a place where the life and people in Brattleboro would shine. I created a formula to keep the column predictably unpredictable. Each month I offered a mix of interests: one historical, one current (tomorrow's history), one editorial, in which our lives of today would be documented, and the other, serendipitous.

The recipe worked. "Downstreet" ran weekly from November 2004 to June 2008. In this collection, I have included only those columns of historical value.

1805 TO 1890s

The Learned Shoemaker of Brattleboro

He was a humble maker of shoes, a trade learned from his father at the age of fourteen at his shop on Main Street. Yet Charles C. Frost—born in town on November 11, 1805, to Brattleboro's first shoemaker, James Frost, and his wife Elizabeth, the daughter of an officer in the American Revolutionary War—had more friends throughout the United States and abroad than he did in the Brattleboro area.

It's possible that two unfortunate circumstances in young Charles's life allowed him to reach his high level of intellect and led him toward his future.

The first came when he was a young student and his teacher struck him with a ruler. He is said to have picked up his books and walked out of the school, determined never to allow anyone to hit him again. Thus he became an apprentice with his father, learning the shoemaking trade.

Frost was already well known for his intelligence, particularly in math. Boys five and nine years older than himself brought their homework to Frost when he was ten, asking for his tutelage. Frost loved to learn, and did so at every opportunity. He studied mathematics, mineralogy, meteorology, astronomy, chemistry, physics and geology, among other subjects, at home. His father came into possession of a book called *Hutton's Mathematics*, which he had taken as payment of a debt from a West Point student. His father challenged him to read it and told him that if he was able to do that by the time he was twenty-one, he could keep the book. Frost threw himself into the challenge.

The second major life change for Frost came when he was diagnosed with dyspepsia, or severe acid indigestion. Not having been cured by any local doctor, he traveled to a specialist in New York. Frost was observed admiring a bouquet of flowers in the doctor's waiting room. After their meeting, the doctor told Frost that there was nothing he could do to help relieve his symptoms, but he said, "You can do very much for yourself. Are you fond of flowers?" Frost agreed. "Then make it a point to walk one hour in the morning and one in the evening, looking for flowers." And he did, with great enthusiasm.

The result was not only the improvement of his health but also the beginnings of studies that would make him an internationally known botanist. Frost devoted himself to his new passion. He purchased a twelve-dollar book on botany from a London dealer, only to find it written in Latin. Undeterred, he studied Latin to learn its contents, and followed with the study of German and French to learn more from other books.

He amassed large collections of mosses, lichens and fungi, wrote a couple of books and painted watercolors of some of his finds. Some of his collection now resides at the University of Vermont. He was given honorary degrees from Dartmouth and Middlebury Colleges and was sought out by many who desired to ask him questions about his studies, including Henry David Thoreau.

Frost remained his humble and practical self. He was not a boastful person or one who sought attention; he simply loved to learn for learning's sake. One visitor wrote after a visit with Frost,

> *On my first visit, which occupied about an hour, we were interrupted six different times. He went to the counter to cut pegs out of the shoes of a factory girl, to sell a pair of slippers to a gentleman for his wife, to ply his trade with one or two country women, etc. He never asked to be excused, but went to his business, came back and resumed just where he left off...I asked him how he could be content to spend his days in that little shoe-shop, with these capabilities and acquirements? He said, "Why, it is the business of my life. Whatever I have acquired of science came in the search of health and mental entertainment. Science is not my profession—shoe making is."*

Who Was Jacob Estey?

From the book *Brattleboro, Biographical Sketches of Some of its Citizens*. by Henry Burnham, first printed in 1880, and long out of print. Here are some excerpts from this book on the life of Jacob Estey.

The families of the name of Estey, are descended from three brothers, who came from England and settled in Massachusetts, early in the seventeenth century. The great-grandfather of Jacob Estey founder and present head of the firm (Estey Organs) also named Jacob, was a farmer in Sutton, MA, but moved early in life to Royalston.

His son Jacob owned and managed a farm in that town, and also kept a public house. Of his seven children, but two attained maturity. The eldest, Isaac, having married Patty Forbes, of Royalston, went with his brother Israel to Hinsdale, NH where they built a sawmill and engaged in the manufacture of lumber. This enterprise was a failure.

Israel Estey left the town and state and went to Ann Arbor, Michigan where he engaged in farming.

His elder brother, Isaac, remaining with his family, was arrested for debt and thrown into the county jail. He remained there thirty days, at the end of which time he took the poor debtor's oath, and was released from his liabilities. He then engaged in farming.

Jacob Estey was one of eight children, seven of whom five sons and two daughters, still survive. He was born September 30, 1814 and was, when four years of age, adopted by a wealthy family in the neighborhood. After remaining with them seven years, he ran away, and walked to Worcester, Massachusetts where a brother lived and where he went to work on a farm.

During the next four years he was employed on farms in Rutland, Millbury and other places in that vicinity. At seventeen he engaged with T&J Sutton of Worcester, as an apprentice to learn the trade of a plumber, including the manufacture of lead pipe.

In February 1835, he went to Brattleboro with two hundred dollars and there purchased the business, tools and real estate of a plumbing and lead pipe concern, and hired a shop on premises opposite the Brattleboro House.

In 1850, the proprietors of a small organ factory, which occupied a part of his building, being unable to pay their rent, he accepted in settlement an interest in the business and two years later purchased the whole establishment which then employed six hands, for $2,700.

Now universally known as one of the foremost businessmen of New England, another subjected to the same conditions, as was Mr. Estey, might have become dissolute, improvident and wretched.

Mr. Estey was married in 1837 to Desdemona Wood, of Brattleboro. Their surviving children are Abby E. born September 21, 1842, and married to Levi K. Fuller, and Julius J. Born January 8 1845 and married to Florence Gray of Cambridge, NY.

Mr. Estey represented the town of Brattleboro in the Vermont Legislature in 1868 and 1869 and the district, including that town in the Senate of 1872 and 1873. He is a director in the Central Vermont Railroad. Mr. Estey is still in the prime of life and retains his business activity. He is a member of the Baptist Church and has contributed freely to religious interest.

In another section, the book details some of the areas of Brattleboro where Estey built his first buildings:

The demand for instruments rendered more room needful, and another larger building was erected south of the bridge in that locality known in early times as "Squabble Hollow." The early names of some of our village localities are not very attractive.

The neighborhood of the "Omnibus" was known as "Polecat" and at the north, where is the Park or Common, "Toad Hill."

How the name of "Squabble Hollow" originated we have not been informed, but we know there was a deadly squabble in one of the old low buildings of this locality in the summer of 1850. There and at that time, Peter Morre in a quarrel with a French Canadian received a fatal stab in the abdomen. By removing the old unsightly buildings and wiping out "Squabble Hollow" Mr. Estey & Co. made an important improvement in this part of the village.

RATTLESNAKE MOUNTAIN

This article appeared in the *Brattleboro Reformer*, August 24, 1883, and was written by Major Frederick W. Childs, correspondent for the *Springfield Republican*. It is edited here for length.

Just across the Connecticut River and directly opposite Brattleboro village, towers old Wantastiquet Mountain. Near its base, and not far from where the zigzag path that leads to the summit begins, may be seen a slide of dirt and broken rock from which stones for building purposes have been taken for a dozen years or so. This ragged place is known by those living on the New Hampshire side as the "rattle-snake den," and wonderful tales are told of its peculiar inhabitants.

Fourteen years ago Andrew D Thomas, then 20 years old, while strolling on the mountain with a friend, accidentally discovered the haunts of these venomous serpents and he thus describes his experience:

"It was Sunday, the next day we had mowed out six rattlers from our hayfield which were stiff and dormant from the effects of the early morning cold. Thinking perhaps we might possibly run upon more we armed ourselves with heavy canes and sauntered out. After walking about the mountain we came across a hole in the ground a trifle smaller than that of a woodchuck. By thrusting our sticks down into it we soon discovered that it was inhabited by snakes, and immediately after we were startled by seeing them all about us, hundreds of them seemingly, coiled on the ground, on stumps, and in fact, up in the bushes. I immediately went to the house, got my gun, and shot 12, which were from two to four feet long. This was the first time they had been discovered in quantities."

Since they have been found there every year by parties who out of curiosity, or with expectations of profit, have searched for them. Mr. Thomas has undoubtedly had the most experience in capturing them, he having caught and sold as many as 100 within the past two years.

One day he brought in eight alive, securing them by a slip-noose made of strong cord and attached to a four-foot stick; these he mostly sold to the local cigar-makers for from $3.50 to $4.50 and as high as $10, who generally

Mount Wantastiquet, taken by Lewis R. Brown from the top of the Wilder Building during the 1930s.

put them in fruit or candy jars filled with alcohol and sent them to New York, but for what purpose he was not appraised.

It is the habit of these snakes to come out of their dens on the approach of warm weather and crawl about the mountain and toward the river until the first cold night, when they gradually work back to their winter quarters. The removing of the stones for the purposes named has served to drive the snakes from their old place of abode to other localities, and they have been found near "Mine Mountain," in the rear of Wantastiquet, and elsewhere.

Mr. Thomas tells of an occasion when he and the late Uncle John Gore were bee hunting near the "mines," when they suddenly came upon three sizeable serpents in the breaks. "Uncle John," being rather poor sighted, nearly stepped on them, but they were finally dispatched and 9 ounces of oil obtained, for which they received $1 an ounce, it being used for croup, rheumatism and other ailments.

Rattle-snakes have often been killed on the road leading from Brattleboro to Hinsdale and in the door-yards of the farmers, though, singularly enough, there have been no fatal snake bites reported within the memory of the present generation, though it is said that a boy was fatally bitten years ago in Chesterfield.

It was not an unusual thing even within a few years past for farmers living near the mountain to take a handful of salt with them whenever they went berrying, which if speedily applied to a bite was believed to be a sure remedy.

An occasional rattlesnake has been killed on the Vermont side of the Connecticut, and these were thought to have swum the river. Royal Wood, who lives but a short distance below the village, killed one not many years ago which was found coiled up on a mat in front of his door. Mr. Thomas declares that the rattlesnakes can be heard from 15 to 20 rods away and that they seldom rattle unless frightened.

BELLS AND CLOCKS

Originally printed in the *Brattleboro Messenger*, January 14, 1832. This article speaks to the clock and bell inside the Center Congregational Church located on the east side of Main Street.

The East Society of this town, having had the misfortune to crack their first bell, lately got up a subscription for a new Bell and Clock, which was soon filled, by rising of eighty subscribers. The bell and clock were accordingly ordered, and brought on by George Holbrook, Esq. and under his superintendence were raised and placed in the tower of the Society. The bell was cast at the foundry of his son, George H. Holbrook of Medway, Mass. and tuned to the letter a gamut of five lines.

This bell is of the first kind of its size; & if it speaks majestically, yet it has something beautiful and sonorous in its sound; and the manufacturer assures us that it will increase in clearness of high sound, more and more delightfully, until it comes to mature age, in five or six years. May it long last, to send its sober melody over the valley, and ascending the hills, remind the good people of the approaching hour of the public worship of the Most High, on the Lord's day.

It is believed there are but few parishes in city or country that would think a bell of 1600 lbs. and a clock of the first order at $400 (none worth more for time, its object) diminutive things, when placed in their towers. We wish every Christian society in the State, the pleasure of these conveniences—and every one might have them if they would unitedly take hold, to get them.

The clock is what is termed horizontal, and is constructed on the best and simplest horological principles for time keeping and durability; it is of the repeating order, and will always strike the hour pointed to, and may be set to the proper hour or minute, almost as readily as a watch; it also has the retaining power, contrived in so plain and simple a manner, that it can be attached to the main wheel in a quarter of a minute, and will lose no time in winding up. Indeed, it looks well, but its main beauty is in its simplicity and strength; there is nothing superfluous about it. In short, it appears well calculated, by the correct time it has kept since it was put up and set going, "to correct old Time and regulate the sun." To be understood as keeping the true mean equated time, agreeing with the sun four times in the year.

It may not be amiss to give a statement of Mr. George H. Holbrook's operations in his business, for the benefit of those who may wish to deal with him, for some of his nice & useful articles. It is believed that his bell foundry is the largest, best conducted, and on the most scientific principles of any in the United States. Mr. Holbrook the elder, before he gave up the business to his son, had been in the constant practice of casting bells for about thirty years, and his inventive mechanical mind led him to try experiments in various ways, forms & sizes of bells, and composition of metals, until he thought he could make no more improvements in the art, and left it as it is, with his son, who now prepares metal enough every week to cast six bells on Saturday, and can cast bells of any size called for up to 10,000 lbs. He also, when requested, pitches a bell to any of the eight notes of the gamut of five lines; of course can furnish chimes of bells when desired.

FIREFIGHTING IN THE NINETEENTH CENTURY

From the *Vermont Phoenix*, December 1, 1848, comes the story of a fire downtown.

About four o'clock Thursday morning, our citizens were aroused by the cry of fire which broke out in Anthony Van Doorn's dwelling on Main Street. That building was soon in flames and also the adjoining Store and House of Mr. Frederick Franks. They were both consumed and nothing by the most strenuous and persevering efforts on the part of Fireman and citizens saved the Phoenix House and probably the whole range of stores and other buildings north of it.

Mr. Van Doorn's house was insured in the Vermont Mutual for about $1,200, and as the building was old, the loss will not be much beyond that amount. The most of his furniture was saved.

Mr. Frank's building was insured for $1,600, in the Aetna Company, of Hartford, which, as his stock and furniture were all saved, will probably cover his loss.

Mr. Charles Fowler, who occupied a part of his building, got his furniture safely out, but suffered some damage from the use of his Carpets to protect the Phoenix House, for which he ought, and doubtless will be fully compensated. Mr. N.H. May was also a tenant, but, as we are informed, saved his furniture.

Mr. James Thompson, Mr. Martin, and Mr. Allen, were also tenants of Mr. Van Doorn.—Mr. Thompson lost considerable furniture, but the others, as we are informed, suffered but little loss.

The Firemen were promptly on the ground with their Engines, and but for an accident which clogged their Engines, it is probable Mr. Frank's building might have been saved.

Fires ravaged Brattleboro many times. Portrayed here is the fire that would level the area again, twenty-one years after the fire described in this article.

Their conduct on the ground was above all praise. Where every one did his duty so faithfully it would be difficult to discriminate; but there were two whose coolness, energy and daring, as they fell under our observation, entitle them to particular mention. Mr. Hinsdale Arms and John Reed, of the Hook and Ladder Company, were conspicuous and foremost wherever the hazard was greatest, and their services most needed.

Our citizens, many of them, responded with alacrity to the call to form lines with buckets, but a considerable number, to their shame be it spoken, lounged with hands in their pockets, in perfect indifference upon the side-walks, refusing every solicitation to lend a helping hand.—they did this when, but for the women, who, now as ever in time of need, stepped forward into the ranks, the lines could not have been extended to the water.

We must not omit our acknowledgments to the Irish laborers on the Rail Road, with Mr. Garvey, their overseer, for their generous and efficient aid. They could not have been more zealous and active if their own houses had been on fire, and they stood to their places while their services were needed. They deserve the thanks of the citizens, and especially of that portion of them, who had nothing else to do, but to admire the splendor of the exhibition.

The public spirited Fire Company in the other village were on the ground with their Engine, and did efficient service, as did also citizens from the neighboring towns.

Our new Engine did wonders; its large and unfailing stream of water, judiciously directed, drove back the flames wherever they broke out on the side next to the Phoenix House. Well may the Company feel proud of her. We have escaped a great disaster by the well directed skill of the fire department, and we saw wanting in it but a Chief Engineer, of requisite influence, firmness and skill, to give to its operations unity and order, as well as efficiency and zeal.

MEDICINE IN THE 1840S

This article first appeared in the *Vermont Phoenix*, November 3, 1848. Dr. Francis John Higginson is writing about a smallpox outbreak in Brattleboro. His story is edited here for length.

On Monday, a young woman who had for several days been ill, presented on her skin appearances, which, taken in connection with the brief history of her case, were sufficient to make the disease as smallpox.

On Tuesday, she was seen by two physicians, one whom has seen all the cases which have occurred in this and the adjoining towns for forty years past, and the other has been at one time in charge of a smallpox hospital. Both agreed in the diagnosis.

On Tuesday morning, the selectmen were called upon to provide for the public safety. The Revised Statutes say: "If any person shall be infected with the smallpox, the selectmen of the town in which such person shall be, shall immediately provide a place as remote from the inhabitants as shall be convenient and remove the person so infected, to such place, unless in the opinion of attending physician the life of such person would be endangered by the removal; and in all cases to take the most prudent measures to prevent the spreading of the disease."

The patient has not been removed, but large placards have been hoisted in the street, wherein is the sick person, at the corners next above and below the house, with "Caution! Small Pox in Elliot Street," in large letters. People are thus to get the disease at their own risk, and if they die, must not find fault with the Selectmen.

Our town authorities have done what seemed to them best, but it does not appear that the public health would be less safe if the notices were fastened on the door of the infected house only, and the alarm excited, would be far less.

The patient occupies a back room and we believe the street a thoroughfare, now, as any in town. The placards themselves were for a whole day eyed askance and our Main Street, though not under ban, was as empty and still as that of a deserted village. Its usual bustle is in some measure restored today.

One person is ill with well-marked smallpox; another is in the same house convalescent from the modified form of the disease called varioloid. Two others were seized at nearly the same time with chills, pains in the head, back and limbs, followed by fever and after a few days with rash upon the skin, but with no distinct pimples, vesicles or pustules. One or two others in the same house have been affected with feverish symptoms, without eruption.

All these individuals were in frequent communication, some in constant attendance on Mrs. H, a lady of our village who has been visiting in New York for 13 days and has been in large crowds.

On Monday following her return home she became sick and a few days afterward an eruption appeared. This lady has had cowpox, and so have all the rest, save her daughter, whose disease has caused all the alarm. It is perhaps proper to state that Mrs. H and three others with the light eruption, have been packed, sweated and bathed, while the daughter has not been so treated.

Smallpox is a severe disease of which people often die, as they do from typhus and scarlet fevers, and from erysipelas (streptococcus bacteria of the skin). Against the terrors of the former, we have the safeguard of vaccination; and a very great, if not perfect one it is.

If it does not remove all susceptibility of smallpox, it in 99 cases out of a hundred, converts a dangerous disease into a safe zone. By avoiding immediate exposure to small pox, and by proper precautions on the part of those in attendance on the sick, the spread of the disease is limited.

Against the three other diseases no such protection is at present known. Yet their presence in a town does not ever excite such unreasonable panic as has been shown about one secluded case of small pox. It certainly becomes the duty of the authorities of the town, while acting under the statute, to endeavor to allay this senseless fear, and carefully avoid all that shall uselessly increase it.

AN EVENING IN BRATTLEBORO

This article originally appeared in the *Vermont Phoenix*, October 16, 1874, and has been edited here for length.

Brattleboro, the guide book tells us, is celebrated for its beautiful scenery, its cultivated and intellectual society, and for its charming and romantic drives and walks. Having very pleasant reminiscences of a short sojourn in Brattleboro some years ago, during which time we made the ascent of Wantastiquet, the mountain that stands overlooking the village like a sentinel; then went away hearing that there were more than twenty drives in the vicinity equally charming. It was with a very cheerful feeling that we found that business would call us thither again.

Late in the afternoon of September 30th, we arrived in town, and after an excellent supper at the Brooks House determined to go up town and make a call. A friendly light from the Brooks House guided our steps for the first few rods but not another light was to be seen.

Preceding northward we very soon found ourselves in total darkness. It was a cloudy night and not a star seen. However, we managed to keep ourselves upon the sidewalk, partly guided by glimmerings from some of the windows of the houses.

All at once we came to a halt rather more suddenly than was agreeable with a violent blow on the forehead, which nearly knocked our hat off and sent us reeling backward.

We found we had run against a large tree, which was growing near the middle of the sidewalk. Standing by the tree an instant to rub our nose and forehead, we were just in the act of re-adjusting our hat and walking on when we heard a light quick step approaching.

Straining our eyes, we saw a shadowy form. Suddenly revealed, a girl rushed past us with a scream evidently frightened half out of her wits, and no doubt concluding we must be some dreadful creature standing behind the tree ready to waylay her.

As her lantern was going in the opposite direction we were soon left in darkness again. We now cautiously resumed our walk, trying to feel our way by the fences, when we heard a carriage approaching, then a sudden crash and a horse dashed violently past us, galloping down the street, then perfect stillness, which in the pitchy darkness seemed frightful. Was any one hurt? There was no scream.

We were trying to make our way toward the spot where the accident occurred when we saw two men issue from a house with a lantern and crossing the street proceed to a pile of lumber and stone that lay on one side of the street, pick up a man who lay there and carry him into the house.

As they took him up, he is limp as though dead, and as they went in and shut the door, I heard the words "seriously injured."

All was now dark again, but the friendly light of the lantern had served to show that we were near the junction of Main and Asylum Streets, (now known as Linden Street) and making a bold dash forward we were just congratulating ourselves upon having crossed the street in safety and thinking we must be near the residence of our friend Gen. Phelps when we found ourselves rolling down a bank into the street which was exceedingly muddy from the recent rains.

Somewhat disconcerted we arose and after groping about for our hat began to meditate upon the probable points of the compass. No friendly lamppost was near, or if near was not lighted, which so far as travelers are concerned amounts to the same thing. Seeing just then a man hanging out a lantern over a gate at a little distance from us we hastened towards it, and found we had retraced our steps and were again on Main Street.

Concluding we had seen enough of Brattleboro for one evening we returned to our hotel, full of thoughts of the dark ages, when there were no street lamps, and feeling glad that we should henceforth know how to appreciate the beauty and blessing of light.

A Curious Fiddle

The story of a fiddle created during the Civil War by a Brattleboro soldier comes from the *Vermont Record*, March 20, 1866. The author of the article is unnamed. It is edited here for length.

Not the least interesting relic of the war that we have seen—one that is most peculiarly blended with the memories of the past—is nothing more nor less than a fiddle. There is no one in Vermont who has not felt its magic power, and who does not associate with its strains the brilliantly lighted ball-room; the array of beauty in all its first ringletted flush and prime; long sleigh rides, thanksgiving dinners, etc., etc. And it is natural that while our boys were lying at Brandy Station, on the Rappahannock, during the gloomy winters of 1864–5, their thoughts should turn towards the more pleasant and festive scenes of their native hills.

"Oh that we had a fiddle!" at length some one exclaimed.

"Well!" said a young farmer from Brattleboro, "I believe boys that I can make you a fiddle."

He had never attempted any thing of the kind in his life.

"Can you?" shouted the boys. "Good! You make one, and we will send to Washington for the strings."

George M. Colt of Company C, 2d Vermont Volunteers, was the one who proposed to make the cheer-giving instrument; and with one hatchet, one jack knife, an old file and a piece of a junk bottle as his only tools, he got a piece of soft maple that grew upon the banks of the Rappahannock, and set to work.

The bottom and side rim of the fiddle are made out of one single piece of maple, in the most approved style and form of the ordinary fiddle. It is a complete dug-out. The top is made of pine. The bow is of maple, the same as the larger part of the shell. The hairs were pulled from the tail of Col. Walbridge's white horse. The glue, some member of the company happened to have with him. And thus, in the course of some five weeks the instrument was completed.

And having been wistfully eyed by the men of the company and regiment for a long time, during its construction, the instrument at length gave forth its stirring strains.

Need we tell how one of their comrades was called out of the hospital to give it a trial—how he played for two hours until he was exhausted—how many stag dances it conjured up—to how many head quarters it went of nights in a round of serenades—how it was admired and cherished by the officers, and wondered at by that prince of tacticians and soldiers—General Getty—what charm of other days in the Green Mountains it threw over the tedious, hard fare and hard duty in camp?

That fiddle is still extant, in all its native simplicity, without paint or varnish, just as it came from the maker's hands, and the writer of this notice has just come from an inspection of it. It is still in the possession of its maker, Mr. George M. Colt, in Brattleboro, who has been pretty severely dealt with by the war, having been wounded no less than five different times, in as many different battles. In the battle of the Wilderness, some two months after the fiddle was completed, he received a wound in the right arm, under which it has withered and stiffened for life.

But still the fiddle goes, and throws its charm over a pleasant household, of which one or two other old veterans of the earlier regiments of Vermont form a part, and where the notes of a seraphine played by a young lady, mingle their harmony with its memory-stirring strains.

More unpretending heroes we have never seen, and a better sounding fiddle has been seldom heard. But amid the joy and hilarity which its harmony awakens, methinks that there is a wail of death—the roar of battle in its sounds. What a glorious instrument to play "Old John Brown!"—made by one of our laboring men of the North, out of Virginia timber from the banks of the Rappahannock, and consecrated by the blood of many battles!

Elm Street Bridge Is Falling Down

This article comes from the *Vermont Phoenix*, February 10, 1888.

There was a surprise party in Brattleboro last Monday morning when it was announced that the Elm Street Bridge across the Whetsone Brook had gone down during the night.

As nearly as can be ascertained it must have fallen about eleven o'clock, and so far as known R.A. Houghton was the last man to cross it.

A few people living near by on Canal Street, heard the noise, but thought it snow falling from some roof. It is evident that the bridge broke at the pier in the middle, and as it fell in the center the two ends, were dragged partly off the abutments. The bridge simply settled down, a mass of broken, splintered timbers, the demoralized roof covering it almost completely.

The bridge was 140 feet long, and though supported by a pier in the center it was built as a single span, the chords being continuous from end to end. The selectmen are satisfied that the weak point was in the chord on the upper or west side of the bridge. One of the three timbers composing the chord had become rotten where it lay on the pier, and it was this, which first gave way. The ends of the bridge were sound, except that the ends of the timbers toward Canal Street had become a little decayed where they lay covered with earth, but not dangerously so.

The bridge was built in June 1873, by Frederick Hawks of Greenfield, the well-known bridge-builder. He examined it last fall, and pronounced it sound and safe, adding that he thought it "about the best bridge he ever built."

Elm Street Bridge, April 9, 1911.

> *His examination was made just before the selectmen had the roof slated at the expense of $235.00. The slate added to the weight of the bridge and there was some accumulation of snow on the roof, but not enough to reach the danger-point if the timbers had been sound. The marvel is that the structure fell of it's own weight and not when a heavy team was crossing it. It is a cause for thanksgiving that it's fall was not accompanied by some shocking disaster to human life.*
>
> *This makes two deliverances of this kind in Brattleboro within a year, the first one being when the bridge on the Book Road fell of its own weight last winter.*
>
> *The selectmen put a force of men at work on the wreck at once, and its removal was substantially completed Wednesday night. More than half of the slate on the roof was saved, and the value of the iron, which is good for use again, is estimated at $100.00.*
>
> *The amount of travel through Elm Street is large, and the selectmen will contract at once for an iron bridge to be erected. It will probably be of substantially the same pattern as that which crosses the brook between Elliot Street and Esteyville.*
>
> *The fate of the Elm Street Bridge has naturally raised a question as to the safety of the West River Bridge, which is also of wood and was built in 1861 or 1862. The selectmen state that they had that bridge examined by Mr. Hawks last year, and he pronounced it sound and safe, as he did the Elm Street one, but recommended that arches, or trusses, be put in within a year or two.*
>
> *The cost of these arches would be $700.00. Since Monday the selectmen have had the snow removed from the roof of the West River Bridge, and their present plan is to order spruce lumber for the arch at once with a view to having them put in as early next spring as possible. The irons taken from the Elm-Street wreck will be good for use there, and will reduce the cost of the arches to $500 or $600.00.*

The current bridge replaced the iron bridge that had replaced the fallen one on Elm Street in the 1960s. Some will remember the bump in the middle of the bridge, which could send occupants in the car out of their seats in the pre–seat belt era.

Eccentric People in Brattleboro Are Nothing New

From *Brattleboro, Biographical Sketches of Some of Its Citizens*, by Henry Burnham, published in 1880.

Mrs. Lydia Child has, in some of her works, compared such person to "sweet bells jangled out of tune."

Such characters of varied capabilities can be found in every community. The great deficiencies in some render them unworthy of notice, but the amusing peculiarities of others cause them to be conspicuous and quite universally known and remembered, while many persons of far greater usefulness are forgotten. Therefore the history of the odd specimens of humanity serves to remind us of persons and events that otherwise would be forever buried in oblivion.

Johnson, the rhymer

Or bard, to whom we have elsewhere alluded more definitely, rarely smiled. Not a day passed when he did not have a grievance, some record of abuse or charge against some one, to send up to the high court of heaven.

Homeless as he was, and wandering in abject poverty from house to house, and passing the long winter nights in a stable, caused some observers of his condition to advise him to apply to the town for relief.

Upon one such occasion he replied, "Don't fret yourself about me. I lodge in a more comfortable place than General Washington did when he was surveying in the forest; and when he was fighting the battles of his country I guess he would have sometimes been glad to find as good a place as Mead's barn to sleep in.

If my shoes do let in the water, there is as good a chance for it to run out as there is for it to get in, and there is as good a chance now for you to mind your own business as there ever will be."

Jimmie Barnes and Sukie, his wife

Our first postmaster found employment for Jimmie Barnes on a farm owned by Mr. Blake in the West River district. At this time Jimmie had no family…Jimmie remained a single man until he met Sukie at the store of John Holbrook in the building now known as the American House. This event must have been before 1810, for Mr. Holbrook ceased his mercantile operations in this place about that time.

From the files of the Brattleboro Historical Society comes this mysterious photo, of what purpose we are unaware.

However much "Barkis was willing," there was a serious objection, in the shape of a husband to be disposed of before Sukie could be honored by the name of Barnes. In all the stores and hotels of that time, customers were furnished with a popular beverage called "flip." This was, we believe, a compound of some kind of ardent spirits, beer, water, nutmeg, sugar and finished by inserting into the mug containing the composition a red-hot iron.

As Esau sold his birthright for a mess of pottage, the husband of Sukie, for a mug of flip, gave up his marital rights to Jimmie and left him in undisturbed possession of "the charmer."

The legality of this affair was never questioned before the courts and for effectiveness, expedition and economy the transaction has never been surpassed, if equaled in this town.

Jimmie ever afterwards had a weakness for the beverage and had as many blessings in store for the man who invented "flip" as Sancho had for the man who invented sleep.

Black Sam

So called, came here from Bennington about 1823 and was at one period the only representative of his race in this place. From that circumstance alone he was conspicuous. He was in the employ of Francis Goodhue, but when he was under the influence of stimulants his employment was less lucrative though much more amusing.

Upon such occasions his powers of imitation were largely developed. The sentiments and exact tones of the voice of his subject were given at the street corners, or wherever he could find an audience. He gave imitations of animals, but he especially delighted in showing off the magnates of Brattleboro; and his patron was not excepted in these laughable exhibitions of his peculiar faculty. Sam was bound to have some fun, and he generally succeeded in accomplishing his object. He did not bind his talent in a napkin, but did all he could to improve his own and other people's digestion.

Built by the residents of the Retreat, Cold Spring can still be seen on the left as one approaches Upper Dummerston Road from Route 30.

AN X-RAY VISION

From the *Vermont Phoenix*, July 14, 1899. .

The Brattleboro Retreat was founded in 1834. A facility for the mentally ill, it was one of the first ten psychiatric hospitals in the United States. Patients were treated in a caring, family-like way with dignity and respect in accordance with a Quaker concept called "moral treatment." This type of atmosphere in a hospital of this kind was greatly different from any other institution of its day. The Retreat was a community all its own and included a working dairy farm from which foods were prepared, a patient newspaper, a gymnasium, a swimming pool and a bowling alley, among other unusual offerings.

> *It was the privilege of half a dozen persons to assemble in the office of the Brattleboro Retreat Wednesday evening to witness a demonstration of a static machine and X-ray attachment, which has recently been bought by the Retreat for use in the treatment of muscular, nervous and other afflictions.*

The occasion was one long to be remembered by all present. The machine is enclosed in an oak frame with glass panels, and it is about five feet high by six feet long and about 2½ feet deep. Its motive power is a water motor located in the basement of the building. The revolving of 10 circular glass plates two feet or more in diameter generates electricity, which is conducted to the positive and negative poles in front of the machine, thereby establishing a circuit.

After the machine was started a Crookes tube was placed in front of it, the poles were separated far enough to break the circuit, and wires, running from the poles, were connected with the ends of the tube causing the electric current to pass through the tube. The Crookes tube is made of glass and is best described by comparing it with a large soap bubble. The tube is almost a vacuum.

As the electric current passed through the tube a brilliant green light was created. This was the X-ray. Dr. Waite then handed a platinum fluoroscope to each of the party, holding his hand between the fluoroscope and the X-ray. The bones of his hand were distinctly visible, much more so than the flesh. One of the party then stood in front of the X-ray while the others looked through his head, saw his jaws open and close, counted his ribs, saw his heart beat, etc.

The fluoroscope was then placed against his shoulder and elbow joints and the movement of the bones was seen. Dr. Waite held a jack-knife in his clenched fist and it could be seen even more clearly than the bones. He then held his foot before the X-ray, showing not only the bones of his foot but the nails in the heel of his shoe.

Photographer John C. Howe, who was present, had with him some sensitive plates, and two exposures were made. A plate was placed on a table beneath the X-ray and the doctor placed his hand upon the plate-holder without removing the slide. The current was turned on for 45 seconds. Absolutely no sensation was felt, but when the plate was developed a perfect negative of the hand and bones was the result.

After this exhibition the X-ray apparatus was removed and a pyrotechnical display was made by the use of the detachable Leyden jars. The display consisted of rapid flashes of electricity, each flash being accompanied by a loud report, which put thunder and lightning "in the shade."

An insulated chair was then placed upon the floor and while the electrical current was passing through it members of the party were invited to sit in it. As they did so their hair rose on end and a delightful electrical breeze was felt. As the lights were turned off halos could be seen around the persons' heads and electric sparks stood on the tip of each hair. One man, who was bald, said the sensation was like rain drops falling on his head. One of the most interesting scenes was when a woman with disheveled hair sat in the chair. Her hair immediately stood out straight from her head for a distance of two feet in all directions.

The purchase of this machine was made to help carry out a plan of the Retreat management to equip its office with the latest and most improved appliances for curing disease. The office was previously equipped with valuable electrical devices, but they covered fields essentially different in character from that which will be attempted by the new machine. Many of the inmates suffering with sciatica, neuralgia, lumbago and kindred afflictions, as well as persons not connected with the institution, have already been benefited by it.

WHO WAS GEORGE CROWELL?

George E. Crowell was born in 1834 in Massachusetts, but he spent the majority of his youth on a farm in Hopkinton, New Hampshire. His father was a farmer and cabinetmaker. George attended the local schools, where he particularly enjoyed literature. At the age of thirteen, Crowell left school and worked the farm with his father during the summer, and in the winter he assisted in the shoemakers shop.

When the Civil War broke out in 1861, twenty-seven-year-old Crowell enlisted for nine months with the Sixteenth New Hampshire Regiment. His company traveled to the Gulf, where he fought in the Louisiana Campaign. While he was away, his father died, leaving him with the deed to the family farm and a heavy mortgage.

When Crowell returned from the war, he decided to go into the newspaper business in an effort to pay that mortgage down. He came to Brattleboro in 1866 to work for the *Vermont Record and Farmer* because he knew the paper's publisher, Daniel L. Millikin. Eventually the newspaper was bought out by the *Phoenix*, precursor to the *Brattleboro Reformer*.

A column in the newspaper was devoted to domestic affairs under the heading "The Household." Readers so loved the original recipes and housekeeping suggestions printed each week that Crowell and Millikin decided to leave their jobs at the newspaper and start their own monthly magazine, which they named after the newspaper column.

The first issue, which contained sixteen pages, was printed in 1868. Despite the *Household*'s initial limited financial success, Crowell bought out his partner and persevered. Seven years later the magazine, which was sold in every state and some foreign countries, was the most popular magazine in the United States. A precursor to the women's magazines of today, it was, at the time, the only magazine devoted entirely to domestic life and boasted a circulation of over eighty thousand. Crowell sold the magazine to a British company in 1890. His publisher went on to found *Good Housekeeping* magazine.

In 1875, Crowell married Mary Louise Spencer, a native of Brattleboro. They had six children, three of whom survived childhood. Among them was Christie B. Crowell, who, in 1926, married local physician Dr. Grace W. Burnett. They divorced eight years later.

Crowell bought the Isaac Hines property, which he renamed Chestnut Hill. There he built an aqueduct system, which became the Chestnut Hill Reservoir. With capacity for five million gallons of water, the reservoir was the town's only water supply. His son Christie managed the business, which was called the Brattleboro Water Works. It was such a success that George Crowell and his son eventually built a larger facility called Pleasant Valley Reservoir, which is still used today. The town of Brattleboro purchased the business from the Crowell family in the 1920s, thus establishing the current town water supply.

Crowell also created a public park on Chestnut Hill, which included a fishing pond, visitors' center and thirty acres of land that he maintained and invited the public to use. At the far end, he built a home, which was run by his wife with the assistance of Mrs. Julius J. Estey. Together they conducted a camp for orphans and invalids on the premises. Eventually Crowell closed the public portion of Chestnut Hill and sold the land for residences.

Crowell also erected a structure on Flat Street that was known as the Jelly Mill. It housed the Brattleboro Jelly Company, which Crowell owned with other investors. The company manufactured cider jelly and cucumber pickles. During the summer, a portion of the building housed fifty Fresh Air children from New York City. Mrs. Crowell, a local doctor and several assistants cared for the children.

George Crowell also owned the Carpenter Company, which manufactured cottage organs on Elliot Street. He sold the business in 1914 when World War I broke out. An enterprising businessman, he also built houses on large tracts of land that he owned in town, with the intention of selling them to middle-class residents.

Mr. and Mrs. Crowell built an elegant mansion called Lindenhurst on the site of the current park.

LINDENHURST AND CROWELL PARK

According to an article in the *Vermont Phoenix* printed in 1895, James B. Eustis, who had served as an ambassador to France and was a U.S. senator from Louisiana, bought land now known as Crowell Park. The purchase included fourteen acres, some of which was pastured land. Eustis improved the house on the property, which had been built as a summer estate, and lived there with his wife.

In 1860, Eustis deeded a two-thirds interest in the property to H.S. Buckner, his father-in-law, who resided in New Orleans. When the Civil War began in 1861—which "was the end of the Southern slaveholders coming North to spend their summers," according to the *Phoenix* article—"Mr. Buckner came near to losing the property under the confiscation act, and only saved it by making over the title to someone else."

George Crowell purchased the property in 1876 and renamed the house Lindenhurst. According to an article from the *Phoenix* dated February 28,

Lindenhurst.

1890, Crowell spent two years rebuilding the house, adding a large number of rooms and several novelties for a late nineteenth-century home—steam heating, gas chandeliers and plate-glass windows. There were lavatories on every floor and on the second and third floors were "well appointed bathrooms." Sixty tons of coal were required to heat the building.

Conservative estimates placed the value of the home at $150,000 in 1890. According to a description of the property from the *Brattleboro Reformer* in 1936,

> *The house itself consists of two parts—the main section surrounded by a wide veranda rising to the third story on the east side, and the ell portion in which was located the kitchen, serving rooms, laundry, shed and servants quarters. There are twenty-seven rooms in the front part of the house and ten in the ell, making thirty-seven rooms in all.*
>
> *An enormous hallway and oak staircase reaching to the four sides of the house on the ground floor and rising through the center of the main section to the observation cupola atop the roof presents an unforgettable impression of the luxuriousness of the building. Expensive grill work and studded ceiling in natural finish combine effectively with the hand-carved woodwork.*

The house boasted fifteen fireplaces, and rooms were furnished in a wide variety of wood, including bird's eye, curly and plain maple, birch, walnut, cherry, oak, ash, frontier mahogany, Tennessee sycamore and gum wood, which came from the sweet gum trees of the South.

Many of the doors were hand done with elaborate carvings, a theme throughout the house. The "reception room" in the front of the home contained a massive fireplace, which sported a carved mantel with the word "Welcome" in the center. As many as twelve varieties of wood were used in a single room.

The Crowell family lived in the home until the late 1920s, George Crowell having died in 1916. In 1934, Lindenhurst became the property of the Vermont Savings Bank in a foreclosure proceeding against his widow, Mary Crowell, her three children and Harold W. Mason, who held a second mortgage against the property. Along with a mortgage of $13,838, $2,541 in back taxes was also due to the town of Brattleboro. The building had been used as a boardinghouse in the interim years.

The bank demolished Lindenhurst and three barns on the property in November 1936. There was no market for a large home, due to the economic downturn of the Great Depression, and no buyer could be found for the acreage, which the bank had hoped to turn into twenty or more building lots. Rather than paying the $400 per year due to the town in taxes, the bank razed the building. At that time the home was valued at $12,000.

Some of the property became Green Street School. In March 1944, the school board borrowed $15,000 and paid the bank for the remaining acres in hopes of building a new high school, which was instead built on Fairground Road. The town-owned land became a playground named in honor of the Crowell family by the board of selectmen. While it is known as Crowell Park today, many residents still refer to the property as the Crowell Lot.

A New Church Is Built on Main Street

According to the book *Brattleboro, Biographical Sketches of Some of Its Citizens* by Henry Burnham, published in 1880, "On account of certain doctrines which he preached, and because he refused to exchange pulpit services with several clergymen with whom Rev. Mr. Wells had been accustomed to hold ministerial intercourse," a group of people who attended the Congregational Society decided to build their own church.

These churchgoers went forth to create the Brattleboro Unitarian Congregational Society in 1831. "The stone church erected…in 1874–1875, surpasses in durability and as a time specimen of church architecture, anything of the kind in this place," states Burnham.

According to the National Register of Historic Places Inventory Nomination Form authored by Hugh Henry of Chester, Vermont, in 1982, Elbridge Boyden of Worcester, Massachusetts, was the architect of the Church and two other buildings on Main Street: the Baptist church and the Brooks House.

Most interesting to me is the feel of the time period during which this church was built. According to Randolph Roth, who wrote a paper called "Can Faith Change the World?" for the Vermont Historical Society in 2001, "Vermonters young and old joined churches by the thousands…By the mid-1830's, Vermonters were the most churchgoing people in the Protestant world. Eighty percent attended church regularly."

With five churches located in the area of Main Street alone, and at the time a population under four thousand people, this fact seems undeniable. But to understand why, one needs to look at society at that time. This was Vermont's great age of reform, when campaigns to end slavery, protect Indian

All Souls Universalist Unitarian Church, August 1903.

rights, improve education, rehabilitate criminals and prohibit the sale and consumption of alcohol were all regular topics of conversation. These reforms were guided, for the most part, through the churches. Traveling preachers went from pulpit to pulpit sharing with small groups of people the faith and political thoughts of other churches and neighborhoods throughout the state.

Nationally, the development of railroads was changing the nation, as well as the face of industry in downtown Brattleboro. The telegraph and the sewing machine had been invented, Walt Whitman was busy shouting poetry to crowds in New York City, Ralph Waldo Emerson had begun his first career as a Unitarian minister and Henry David Thoreau was living on Walden Pond.

In 1852, Jacob Estey bought an interest in a small company making melodeons and within twenty years would be the largest manufacturer of organs in the world. With the advent of railway service in Brattleboro, any location on the globe could purchase organs from Brattleboro, Vermont.

This industrial age brought dramatic redevelopment to our Main Street, creating the blueprint for its current look. The First Baptist Society built its church in 1867, just two years after the Civil War, and a local historian judged the building as "the most costly and elegant specimen of church architecture this side of Rutland, if not in the State."

In October 1869, a flash flood along the Whetstone Brook caused $300,000 worth of damage in the town, and later in the month a fire burned the entire west side of Main Street between Elliot and High Streets. New buildings appeared from the rubble.

Imagine what it felt like to be a citizen of Brattleboro during these times. The sounds of hammering, sawing and the yelling of one workman to another—many of whom were immigrants—along Main Street must have been constant. Women's hooped skirts floated above the cobblestone streets as the ladies walked between the shops. Horses were tethered to granite posts beside the street. The clippity-clop of horseshoes rang out as wagons and carriages carted animal feed and merchandise to farms as far away as Marlboro, a full day's ride.

HANDCRAFTED MASTERPIECE

While I do have some documents written about the architecture of the former All Souls Universalist Unitarian Church (currently privately owned and referred to as "The Church"), I am left to draw my own conclusions about how the building was actually made.

The sources I located acquainted me with the construction of cathedrals in the Middle Ages between the 1200s and 1300s, when the majority of these enormous church buildings were erected in Europe. Sometimes it took two hundred years to build them.

The Church in Brattleboro was constructed between 1874 and 1875 at a cost of $40,000. Its architect was Elbridge Boyden of Worcester, Massachusetts, a Vermont native. Boyden was also the designer of the Brooks House and the First Baptist Church, all of which were built along Main Street during a span of about ten years.

The Church is an impressive illustration of the High Victorian Gothic style. According to the National Register of Historic Places Nomination Form authored in 1982 by Hugh Henry, "Its walls and northeast corner tower are built of polychrome quartzite rubble laid up in random courses and trimmed with hand-carved pale granite. The steeply pitched roof is shingled with slate." I believe the word "rubble" is used only because each individual stone was not cut to fit by a stonemason.

Research tells me that the site would have been laid out with wooden stakes and laborers would have begun the process of digging the basement. There were likely large numbers of people working on the project since it needed to be accomplished by hand and was complete within two years. It is likely that the craftsmen would have included a master quarryman, a master stonecutter, a master sculptor, a master mortar maker, a master mason, a master carpenter, a master blacksmith, a master roofer and a master glassmaker.

Each master craftsman would have run his own workshop for his trade, and each would have had many apprentices who were in the process of learning the trade in hopes of becoming masters themselves at some point and opening their own shops. Laborers probably did most of the heavy lifting and digging; these were people with no particular skills, many of whom I feel sure were immigrants to this country.

Local stones taken from the quarry at the foot of Wantastiquet were likely floated across the Connecticut, moved to carts and pulled by horses to the site of construction. The basement of the Church needed to be sturdy, deep and vast to assume the massive weight of the structure. It was imperative that the master mason check his level often to be sure that once the basement was complete the building would be square. Stones were placed; the mortar men were ready with exact mixtures of sand, lime and water; and the masons would lay the stones on top of one another, toweling mortar between each layer of rock.

Meanwhile, wood for the interior timbers was probably cut nearby. The Church features an exposed ceiling supported by ribbed rafter beams and arches, a paneled front and wainscoting below the windows.

The key to the height of the building was plausibly a windlass, an apparatus for moving the heavy stones and timbers. A wooden barrel was attached to a crank that turned it around. A winch attached to the barrel, and rope was fastened to the winch that would pull up a weight on the opposite end.

Windlasses were moved up scaffolding built beside the church walls so that stone could be lifted into place. The same method was probably used to lift the cross to the top of the steeple.

I'm surprised that the building was finished in just two years, as it was of the utmost importance to allow the cement to dry completely before proceeding with the height of the walls. That tells me that laborers continued working through the winter with some sort of heating inside the building; otherwise the cement would not have dried.

The stained glass was installed by Baker and Son of New York and illustrates the Life of Christ. W.J. McPherson of Boston painted interior murals, and some Swedish parishioners who were employed at the Estey Organ Company created floral stenciling. These features have been preserved.

Main Street, Brattleboro, 1916.

THE IRISH IN BRATTLEBORO

Edward Baker Square

Bridget Griffin Baker arrived in Brattleboro from Dingle, Ireland, when she was sixteen years old, in 1889. Her grandson, Steve Baker, owner of Baker's Business Interiors and Baker's Hallmark, recalled recently how much his Grandmother Bridget enjoyed visiting Hampton Beach on the New Hampshire coast. "It reminded her of Dingle," he said.

Bridget's in-laws owned three houses on Elliot Street where a majority of Brattleboro's Irish immigrants lived. Her mother-in-law, Hannah, gave Bridget and her husband, Michael Baker, the opportunity to live at the former 146 Elliot Street for a lifetime tenancy for one dollar. Their nine children were born in the house where originally there was no central heating and Bridget cooked all of her family's food on a wood stove in the kitchen.

Steve Baker's father, James, grew up in the household. He remembered, "My father told me that my grandparents were thrifty people. If they had beet greens in the garden, the kids were fed beet greens for breakfast, lunch and dinner."

The eldest of Bridget and Michael's children was named Edward M. Baker, born May 10, 1901. He was Steve Baker's uncle. "My Uncle Edward had to get permission from his parents to enlist in the army when he was fifteen years old. Prior to that he attended St. Michael's prep school for junior high and high school, which later became St. Michael's College in Winooski, Vermont," recalled Steve.

The year 1916 found young Edward a private in the army, serving on the Mexican border with other Brattleboro boys Jim Denning, Ernie Johnson

Welcome Home Parade for World War I soldiers.

E. E. PERRY & Co.
5 AND 10 CENT STORE

and Bernard Dunlevey. The revolutionary Mexican general Pancho Villa, allegedly sponsored by the Germans who were already engaged in World War I, launched a raid and captured nineteen U.S. citizens in January 1916. "The Brattleboro boys ended up chasing Pancho Villa," said Steve.

In 1917, when the United States officially entered World War I, the *Brattleboro Daily Reformer* reported on April 3, 1917, "This morning at six o'clock the first alarm sounded the ten blows of the military call and from all over town members of the company were soon hurrying towards the Armory [now known as the Gibson-Aiken Center]."

Baker's company was shipped to France. He was a private in the 103rd Company, 26th Division, of the American expeditionary force, along with 101 other young men from Brattleboro.

Edward Baker died February 28, 1918, at the tender age of sixteen. He was the first Brattleboro citizen to die during World War I. It is not known whether he perished in the flu epidemic or if his appendix burst, but the *Brattleboro Daily Reformer* reported in the evening edition on March 12, 1918, "Although he did not die in actual engagement his death none the less was for you and me, that our homes might be saved. God met the supreme test of love by giving the life of his son to save the world. Young Baker met the supreme test of love by giving his life to save his country."

Edward's funeral service was held at St. Michael's Catholic Church. An audience that almost filled the church attended the service. The altar was draped in mourning and on either side was the Stars and Stripes. Although his body was in France, the ceremony was carried out as though it had been present.

Reverend James P. Rand, who continued to serve his church community for over fifty years, gave the eulogy. Edward Baker is interred in St. Michael's cemetery south of the Reverend Cunningham circle.

Several years later, a bronze memorial plaque featuring a star atop the words "Edward Baker Square" was placed in the small park at the corner of Church and Green Streets in honor of young Baker's sacrifice. Many years later, the Brattleboro American Legion Post decided to remove the memorial and replace it on the square at Park Place and Putney Road so that it could be more visible in the community. The marker can still be seen as the road splits to the roundabout and up Putney Road, and it is marked by an American flag.

"He died when he was almost seventeen, but at that time he'd already served in the army for close to two years," said Steve Baker. "My grandmother didn't talk about him much. I imagine it was terribly difficult to lose her eldest son to war."

The Irish on Elliot Street

"'If you stand on the shore in County Kerry, you can see the ports of Boston.' That's what my father told me my grandfather always said," commented Brattleboro's proud Irishman, Timothy O'Connor.

O'Connor's grandparents each came from County Kerry, arriving in the United States in 1895. But they never met each other until they each found themselves in Norwich, Connecticut, he working in a local paper mill, and she working as a domestic at a local hotel. The pair met, married and moved to Bellows Falls, where relatives had secured jobs for them in a local paper mill.

A few years later, O'Connor's grandparents moved to Putney to work in the paper mill there and to raise their children—two girls and two boys. A few more years passed and the clan journeyed to Brattleboro. Timothy Patrick O'Connor worked at the Vinton Paper Company located behind what is now the Brattleboro Food Co-Op, and Hannah Daly O'Connor worked as a domestic for the Estey family.

O'Connor remembered,

> *At first, my father, also named Timothy James O'Connor, lived over on Reed Street and then they moved to Elliot Street where the majority of the Irish families in town lived at that time. Unfortunately my grandfather was killed in an industrial accident in 1915, and just seven years later, my grandmother died of consumption, what we now know as tuberculosis.*
>
> *The Irish on Elliot Street were a close bunch though, and Richard and Hanna Hasey took my father in and raised him as their own since he was the youngest and they didn't want him to have to go to an orphanage. My father went to Bentley School of accounting and finance in Boston and worked for Barrows Coal Company for forty-eight years.*

There were lots of good folks in that small Irish community, plenty of names in Brattleboro that started there in that first generation of Irish immigrants. There was the Flynn family, the Heapheys, the Danyews and Jim and Thomas Guiheen; they worked over at E.H. Hildreth's printing shop. Tom Lynch, who was on the town planning commission, had family on Elliot Street, along with Bob Manning, who worked for many years in the Brattleboro Post Office. Of course there was the Baker family that now own their stores in town, and Patrick Fleming, his son Richard started Fleming Oil, and his other son Joseph started Fleming's Funeral Home. And we can't forget Dr. William Kaine, he delivered me.

Some of the Irish came with few skills, but many came as stonemasons, jobs they had held in Ireland. The local Irish stonemasons built the All Souls Church on Main Street, including the Celtic cross that can still be seen on the church lawn.

Looking west on Elliot Street.

O'Connor recalls,

> *As a lawyer, assisting local people with old deeds to property, I would occasionally see, when I first started working, deeds from the last twenty-five years of the 1800s that included restrictions that "property shall not be sold to Irish citizens." It was like the old signs in windows that said, "No Irish need apply." After that first generation, Irishmen assimilated into our culture, and the second and third generations melted into the community and weren't as visible as they once were.*
>
> *When I was a kid at St. Michael's School, every St. Patrick's Day all the classes would participate in a show. The band would play and the classes would each sing the old Irish songs. It was a day for talking about St. Patrick, who established Christianity and is the patron Saint of Ireland. And we still pay homage in that way. Monsignor Father John Rand started the traditional St. Patty's Day supper at St. Michaels in the early 1900s, something we continue to this day.*

More Irish

Mrs. Margaret Borkowski has been a resident of Guilford since her husband John took her as his wife in 1940. Prior to that, Borkowski always lived with her parents in Brattleboro. Here are some of her memories of life around town in the old days.

> *My parents were Irish immigrants, my mother from Dingle in County Kerry Ireland, and my father came from County Cork, same as Mrs. Baker and Mrs. O'Connor. My mother, Margaret Fitzgerald, was considered an old maid since she was thirty-four and unmarried. My father Jim Lyons was also unmarried and was thirty-four as well. They met at a dance on Island Park* [the area of land in the middle of the Connecticut River, where famous dance bands of the day often played in the ballroom].
>
> *After they were married, my father built the apartment building at the former 214 Elliot Street. He was a successful man, but came from a poor background. My parents felt fortunate that they could build such a fine building. I admire my parents; they had a lot of courage.*
>
> *The building was three stories and white at the time it was built. There were four children in our family, and there was a five-room*

apartment upstairs, but my parents felt that those we rented to should have the bigger space, so we lived in the four-room apartment in the basement.

I was born in 1917 and attended school at St. Michael's. I would walk down the street each day, and on the corner of Elliot and Main, Patrick O'Keefe, the police chief, was always there. He looked out for all the kids in town, and my mother knew that he was a good man and wouldn't ever let anything happen to her children. My parents were happy to have a family late in life. They were very protective of all of us.

My father worked with stone in Ireland and started a business on South Main Street selling sand, gravel and cement blocks. Eventually that business was sold, but it is still there at the foot of Fairground Road and is owned by Whitcomb from Keene.

The following year, he purchased a house that was on the property where the Little League ball field is now located. It was a falling-down sort of house, but my father bought some property from Farmer Bailey, put in a cement foundation for it and hired the Gallops from Guilford to haul it up the hill on blocks to the corner of Clark Avenue and Moreland Avenue and rebuilt the place. It's a very sweet little house and sits there still. He also built Mary Ryan's place at 49 Clark Avenue, and John Gagnon's house, number 33.

Farmer Bailey was a big guy, and used to wrestle professionally. He was a wonderful man, and everyone loved him. He owned the house on Canal Street that now belongs to Planned Parenthood, and where the gas station is now located next door, he had a large plot of land where he grew his flowers. His good friend Laddie Allen often went horseback riding down Clark Avenue.

That area of town had a lot of building going on then. The cotton mill had come in from Rhode Island and so many of the workers needed housing and wanted a place to live close by. George Houghton, George Holden and my father would build one house every winter. My father did the cement work and one George would build most of the outside and the other George would build most of the inside. They built houses all over Clark, Moreland and Oak Grove Avenues. The two Georges went on to build all the homes on Home Street and many others in the area.

When my father died in 1950, so many people told me stories of kind things he had done for them. At the time, if you wanted to build a home, you had to purchase the land and put in your stonework for the cellar. After that was done, you went to the bank and borrowed the money for the house. The Mellish family told me that they didn't have much, but had wanted to build a home, and that my father had quietly done their cement work for free. He had never told us that. That's who he was. He was often quietly helping others simply because he could.

THE ERA OF THE GREAT DEPRESSION

From 1929 forward, the Works Progress Administration (WPA) and the National Recovery Act (NRA) provided an entire alphabet soup of federal programs to help America get back on its feet following the stock market crash. Brattleboro participated in most of the federal projects.

If you needed a job, you went to visit Town Selectman Jason Bushnell, who was in charge of the local WPA. Women had a choice of two jobs: sewing pajamas for youngsters without or updating school records. Men had more of a choice, but positions within the Civilian Conservation Corps (CCC) were popular jobs. The CCC involved building state parks and roads or planting trees. Both the men and the women were paid fourteen dollars every two weeks for their work.

Brattleboro was also involved in the WPA project of making a guidebook for the area. After a few hundred copies were published, the blocks were destroyed, making them worth hundreds of dollars today. An updated copy of this book may be obtained at the Brooks Memorial Library. It is called *Vermont Federal Writer's Project*.

Businesses were forced to comply with WPA wage standards. Mr. Joseph Juscen worked at Berkshire Fine Spinning Mill, located at the site of Cotton Mill Hill. Before the WPA was introduced, his millworker employment consisted of a fifty-six-hour workweek. After the new federal laws, he worked only forty hours per week and was paid thirteen dollars every two weeks.

Berkshire Fine Spinning took its money out of the bank before the bank holiday, making workers eligible for pay by cash instead of check, a helpful thing since the banks were closed for ten days. Mr. Juscen remembered, "The only place you could cash a check was Jim Galanes's store."

In town, people received their money back from the bank in seven or eight years, but customers of the Brattleboro Trust Company got 50 percent of their savings back in bank stock. Mrs. Emily Harriet Chapin Wright, who lived in West Brattleboro but kept her money in a Massachusetts bank, received only 25 percent of her money back from her bank.

Mrs. Jenny Russell remembered, "Everything was cheap." A gallon of kerosene was fifteen cents; a tank of gas to fill your Model T was twenty cents. Meat, ten cents a pound; apartment rent, fifteen dollars a month, eighteen dollars to rent an entire house; bread from the Dutch Bake Shop, a few cents a loaf; dinner at a local restaurant, twenty-five cents; candy, five cents a bag. A Maytag washing machine cost seventy-eight dollars. An operation on a local boy in Boston cost seventy-five dollars. A special night nurse cost an extra five dollars plus the cost of her meals.

A. Chapin Wright was commander of the Brattleboro chapter of the American Legion during the Depression years. "I received a report that three people were starving to death in the country. All that they had to eat was some milk from a farmer up the road. We did our best to take care of

Latchis Fruit Store, lower Main Street, Brattleboro.

them. Mortgage payments were hard to make. Some people had to choose between keeping their home and feeding their families."

Banks repossessed plenty of homes. Out of the forty or so houses located on Clark Street at the time, there were only two that the bank did not repossess.

Still, when asked if Brattleboro was hit as hard as the cities, most of those interviewed said no. Mr. Wright remembered, "Brattleboro was a community of farmers. We weren't hit as bad as the cities because we could trade homemade items for what we didn't have, and we grew our own food. Lots of people traded butter for eggs, that sort of thing." Mr. Wright remembered trading four sheep for a used car.

Though the full impact of the crash would be seen in bold type in future *Brattleboro Reformers*, the headline on October 29, 1929, the day of the stock market crash, read, "Bennington Trout Victims of Drought."

An earnest kid could make an honest penny in Brattleboro during the Great Depression. Many Brattleboro boys did this by selling copies of the *Brattleboro Reformer*. "We bought 'em at two cents and sold 'em for three cents. When you'd sold five hundred papers, the *Reformer* would give you a dollar or a dictionary. Most of the kids would take the dictionary first, and then the dollar," remembered Clarence Fairchild.

Other businesses in Brattleboro did what they could to stay afloat and hire as many people as they were able. Some local businesses included Betterley & Avery Chevrolet Company on Canal Street (where Walgreens now stands), run by Mr. John Avery; Hotel Billings (where the Food Coop stands); and Crystal Springs Ice Company on Frost Street, owned and operated by Henry Whitney, one of Brattleboro's town selectmen.

Mrs. Janice Wright Bodor described businesses in town from a child's perspective:

> *Mr. Stockwell ran the grocery store in West Brattleboro and also was the barber in the barbershop next door where the West Brattleboro Post Office was. Mr. Stockwell had a thick white drooping moustache.*
>
> *There was West Brattleboro Grist Mill, which was a feed store. Robert Underwood's father was the boss there, and he'd let us ride on top of the bags of grain on the flatbed truck during deliveries. Behind the gristmill was a swinging footbridge, which was a pretty scary way to cross the Whetstone* [from Western Avenue to the Melrose Terrace area]. *In Centerville, opposite LaRose's Country Store* [now known as Vermont Country Market and Deli] *was a little white shed where*

Island Park, seen here (left), washed away for the second time in the flood of 1936. Cement footings can still be seen today.

Mr. Pratt caned chair seats. The Brattleboro Riding Stable used to be at the corner of Western Avenue and Orchard Street all the way into the forties.

Despite hard times, money was willingly spent on entertainment. The Valley Fair came around once a year and lasted three long, exciting days. It was held on Fairground Road where the high school stands today. Dances were held in the town hall on Main Street, where Candle in the Night is currently located. A horse show was held occasionally on the field behind Mr. Pratt's shed at the corner of Brattle Street. (The interstate runs over this land.)

You could visit Island Park, which was located in the middle of the Connecticut River. The land was eventually washed away during the Hurricane of 1938. Island Park had pony rides, places to rent a boat, sled races on the river in the winter, baseball games and outdoor movies. The high school football team played its games on the island for lack of a playing field.

In Brattleboro, movies cost ten cents. Wednesday and Thursday were double-feature days, when two movies could be enjoyed for fifteen cents.

Mrs. Jenny Russell remembered, "There was such a fly problem in Brattleboro, movie theatre owners would let kids in early to catch the flies. If you could catch fifty flies in a glass jar before the show, you would receive free admission in return."

The state of Vermont didn't allow movies to be shown on Sundays, so people went to Island Park to view them instead, as the park itself fell under New Hampshire law. Outdoor movies were shown over home plate. People would sit in the bleachers to view them.

If you wanted to get around Brattleboro, you took the trolley. The trolley ran the same route as the town bus does today. It cost a dime to ride. If you owned a car, it was probably black, boxy and had a running board. Seats were gray plush, with a long gear shifter running from your knee to the floor.

Concerning Prohibition, Brattleboro was a dry town, but Greenfield, Massachusetts, was wet. Consequently, some would take a train from Brattleboro to Greenfield or from New Hampshire to Brattleboro to Greenfield for a drink.

The majority of those whom I interviewed agreed with A. Chapin Wright's statement concerning the Depression years in Brattleboro: "I guess, when I think about it, the children of the era came out okay and weren't especially affected by it. At least in the northeastern part of the USA or in 'the country' if you had a garden and a roof over your head, you could get by during the truly difficult years."

PATRICK J. O'KEEFE

In the 1930s, Green Street was closed in the winter during snowstorms between the hours of 3:30 and 9:00 p.m. to accommodate sledding. It was during the Great Depression, and many children lived without the luxury of sleds, using cardboard boxes instead.

Elnora "Nonie" Ward Ripchick recalls,

> *Everybody in town slid down that hill. Pat O'Keefe was a local police officer and he took a shine to my little brother Bill. Pat knew we often did without extras. One day, he brought my sisters and Bill to Emerson's, where they sold sleds. He had Bill pick the one that he liked the best and bought it for him. As we left the store, Pat put his hand on Bill's shoulder and said, "Billy, you steer it and don't let those girls fall off."*
>
> *He was a fatherly figure to everybody, but he also let us know when we were wrong.*

"Pat O'Keefe had a big heart, and was very friendly," remembers Cynthia Fairchild. "He often filled his car with kids to go to a square dance, especially young women who had no escorts. He'd put on his police hat, become officer of the peace while he was at the dance and then he'd bring the kids home."

Patrick J. O'Keefe was born in 1889 in Taunton, Massachusetts, and died in Brattleboro sixty-two years later, in 1951. He spent time in the Merchant Marines during World War I and then worked as a police officer in White River Junction, eventually becoming chief of the department. In 1923, he was hired as chief of police in Brattleboro. His work in that position gained him such respectability in Windham County that after several years he ran for county sheriff. In succeeding elections, Sheriff O'Keefe often received the largest number of votes cast for any county officer. O'Keefe was one of the most known and respected members of the police force in Vermont.

His obituary printed in the *Brattleboro Reformer* states, "In his nearly eight years as police chief he was off duty less than a month, worked seven days a week and did not take a single day off because of illness."

Patrick J. O'Keefe, chief of police. *Courtesy of the family of Jenny Russell.*

"He had an endless supply of chewing gum in his pocket and asked to look at kids' report cards," remembers former Brattleboro police chief Richard Guthrie, who grew up on South Main Street. "He knew the names of every kid in town. I was proud of the fact that he knew me. He created great trust in law enforcement. Looking back on my career, he was a positive influence. You always knew where to find him if you needed him."

Pat O'Keefe also knew where to find everyone he was looking for in his position as an officer of the court. There were no police cruisers at the time, so O'Keefe had a walking beat. He could often be found at the corner of Elliot and Main, next to the former Vermont National Bank.

"He kept his briefcase inside the bank," Guthrie remembers. "In it, he kept all the paperwork he needed to serve to people. Eventually, he'd see anyone he needed to find."

Attire for law enforcement was plain clothes. "He was a sharp dresser. He set the tone for the spring and summer. You knew it was spring when he put on his straw hat, and you knew winter was coming when he put on his fedora," laughed Guthrie. "No one knew much about him personally though and that made him a good cop. He was standoffish about himself, but had a humanistic approach to everyone."

"I never knew he was bald until his funeral, because I never saw him without his hat," commented Peg Barry.

He worked until a few months before his death, due to illness. Stories of him abound to this day: the matinee tickets he purchased for kids who couldn't afford them, the jobs he found for drifters who came through town looking for work, the fireworks and watermelon he quietly left on the porch of a family who were under quarantine all summer due to scarlet fever. His good deeds and kindnesses are legendary.

"He helped so many people," said Pauline Searles Corey. "My mother used to think he was the greatest man on earth."

Flying High on Harris Hill

Hometown boy Merrill "Mezzy" Barber became an honorary citizen of Norway and was inducted into the Ski Jumping Hall of Fame in 1999. But his passion for ski jumping began in the 1930s. His family decided that he ought to be living in Norway, where he could learn the sport where it originated, so he boarded a steamship and headed across the ocean.

Meanwhile, in Norway, Toger Tokle, referred to as "the Babe Ruth of ski jumping," was cutting his teeth on the sport that would intersect with Mezzy Barber's life many times. And over on Myrtle Street, a young boy named Richard "Tink" Austin was building jumps on Haskell Hill, which borders Spruce Street. He adored the speed and the feeling of flying. He started out airborne in cardboard boxes when he was less than ten years old.

Harris Hill Ski Jump, 1920s.

Harris Hill Ski Jump on Cedar Street eventually brought these men, and many more, together. Fred Harris decided that Brattleboro should be part of the ski jumping mania that gripped the United States in 1922 and proposed building what became Harris Hill. The price of the wooden structure was $2,000. At the hill's inauguration in 1923, the entire cost was recouped in one day as thousands of people came to view the National Ski Jumping Championships.

Tink Austin was smitten with the sport.

> *I went from flying on toboggans as a kid, to co-piloting a B-17 bomber in Europe. I flew thirty-five missions over Europe in the Eighth Air Force. When I got home, I went right back to ski jumping and flying through the air. My first jumping skis were used and cost three dollars. One was six inches shorter than the other.*
>
> *Ski jumping was* the *sport in the 1930s, '40s and '50s. I won the high school championships in 1941, and my son David won it thirty years later. There was a bunch of us who loved to jump so much we'd drive anywhere to do it. But having Harris Hill in our own backyard was a great thing. To jump, the hill has to be packed with snow. Every time it snowed we'd side step the hill over and over to pack the fresh snow down. Sometimes it took us all day to pack it and we'd only get in a run or two, but it was worth it to us.*

Years later, in the mid-1960s, Mezzy Barber's nephew Hugh took up the sport at the age of thirteen. "I learned to ski jump from my Uncle Mezzy. I jumped Harris Hill, Maple Valley, Bear Mountain over in New York and Lake Placid to start," says Barber.

Hugh went on to Middlebury College and learned a great deal from his college coach. Eventually, he jumped all over the nation. By 1972, he had already retired the winged trophy at Harris Hill as his Uncle Mezzy and Torger Tokle had done before him, won the Carnival Circuit Championship (a jumping competition involving Middlebury, Dartmouth, St. Lawrence and Williams Colleges) and come in seventh at the NCAA Championships in Deadwood, South Dakota.

"I could have done better, but I was jumping with pneumonia and was in the hospital during a few days of the contest," says Barber.

"But the first hill of them all," Barber said, "is Harris Hill. All the competitors enjoy it. It's got speed, excitement and plenty of air pressure. Some hills are not sited as favorably as Harris Hill. Hopefully that hill will come alive again. It's not only our local history, it's still a great place to jump."

For Hugh Barber, his happiest jumping experiences came when people in the crowd would recognize his name and ask him if he was related to Mezzy Barber.

"Mezzy was a terrific competitor. He was the first guy in North America to jump three hundred feet. He was a nice person and was loved by everybody. I was proud to say that I was his nephew," said Barber.

The Old Ballgame

In 1939, baseball was in the news. Ted Williams hit his first home run in the Major Leagues at Fenway Park. Lou Gehrig voluntarily benched himself "for the good of the team," ending a consecutive 2,130-game career. The greatest lineup in the history of baseball arrived in Cooperstown, New York, for the dedication of the Baseball Hall of Fame. Babe Ruth, Ty Cobb, Cy Young, Honus Wagner and Walter Johnson all played at the event.

And over in Guilford, Vermont, the locals were rooting for the hometown team to beat their rival, Jacksonville, in the West River League. The league involved the towns of Wardsboro, Wilmington, South Newfane, Townshend, Jacksonville and Guilford.

Left fielder Robert Gaines recalls,

> *At the time, there were only about three hundred residents in Guilford. In those days, you didn't really meet other boys in town until you went to high school. We all went to one-room schoolhouses all over Guilford.*
>
> *The average age of the players was probably around twenty-five, maybe a little bit older. I was lucky. I was able to join the team at eighteen because I had played ball for Brattleboro High School, but I was one of the younger ones. Every team had a limited number of players to draw from, but everybody wanted to play. It wasn't just a Sunday get-together; all of the teams really wanted to win the season.*
>
> *Herman Ashworth was the manager. Ray Ashworth played first base. His brother Bob played shortstop. Francis Hastings was catcher. His wife was sister to the Ashworth boys. Leon and Charlie Ogden were both pitchers and outfielders. One week one pitched and the next week they switched places. Cy Tracy played center field. Freddie Bowen, who came over from Halifax, played third base. Most of the team lived on family farms.*
>
> *It was quite a trek to the games. The first game I didn't have any transportation so I walked to Algiers to meet someone to give me a ride. I was so happy to be playing, I didn't mind the five-mile walk.*

We didn't exactly have the ideal ball field. It was actually one of the pastures on the Ashworth Farm. We had to shovel the infield every Sunday. It was pretty level on the infield, but left field dropped way off. From the back of it, you couldn't even see the catcher.

We were a lucky bunch. The other town teams had to get sponsors to buy their uniforms. Most asked their local gas station to do it. We had a man we called One-Armed Bennett. He was a retired big league ballplayer. He bought our uniforms for us, and he was always at the game. He was a booster for the team, a real supporter.

Our uniforms were blue and white. We had blue stockings with a white ring around them, and we wore blue caps. There were letters on the front that said "Guilford" and there were numbers on the back. In those days you didn't put the name of the player on the uniform.

Alicia Ogden Thomas was the scorekeeper.

My husband Leon Ogden loved baseball and kind of volunteered me to keep the scores. I did all the bookwork, kept the batting averages and the schedule of all the games. We had two sons. The oldest was five and the youngest was a baby. We bundled him up and took him to all the games. Every single Sunday we were with the team. We started in the spring with practice and played until Labor Day.

"Jacksonville had a good team, no question about it," said Gaines. "We were nip and tuck between the two teams throughout the season. As I remember it, we were winning and on that last game we took the championship because Jacksonville lost the game. We didn't need to have a playoff."

By 1941, the league had disbanded. "Most of the guys joined the service," said Gaines. "But we all had a lot of fun. Baseball was something to look forward to. Entertainment in those days wasn't what it is today."

THE REED STREET KIDS

Located off the southern end of South Main Street, Reed Street now serves as a parking lot for the Holstein Friesian. Named for the family of Frank Reed, who settled in the area in the 1700s, Reed Street once had as many as twenty-five multifamily homes squeezed onto its tiny hillside. During the late 1870s, there were enough children on the hill to warrant its own schoolhouse.

In January 1913, the Boston & Maine Railroad reorganized Reed Street in an effort to provide more housing to its workers. "15 new tenements added which include bathrooms and electric lights," bragged a news release. Most of the neighborhood was filled with Irish immigrants who worked the railroad.

By the 1930s, Reed Street housed more than twenty-five families, each family unit averaging four children. It was a harsh existence during the Great Depression. Jobs were scarce. Mothers headed some families as fathers left the area looking for work. A baby was left in a closet to die because the family didn't have the food to keep it alive. Eventually, authorities found the child and the father was hauled off to jail.

Still, families stuck together and formed tight bonds, especially the children of the neighborhood. Since houses were packed tightly, there was little space for children to play.

"We played one potato two potato, kick the can, hide and seek, it didn't take much to keep us kids occupied," commented Gerry Searles Harrington, now of Newfane, who grew up on Reed Street along with her two brothers and four sisters in the 1930s and '40s. "Reed Street was a tough street but it made all the kids in the neighborhood close. We all stuck together."

Most of the houses came down in the 1950s and '60s to make room for the expansion of the Holstein Friesian. The Community Land Trust revitalized the few remaining.

As she watched the neighborhood drastically change over the years, Gerry wondered what became of her playmates from Reed Street. In 1992, she called all the old neighbors she could think of and invited them to meet for a Reed Street Kids Reunion in September. Twenty-three "kids" came that first year, representing eight families.

"This is history. We're the only street in Brattleboro that does this. We swap stories, keep our friendships alive and catch up every year," remarked Gerry.

The "Kids" have enthusiastically taken on the job of documenting their shared history. Each member has filled out a worksheet, which chronicles stories of the past and shares news of how each "kid" turned out. Some have included pictures from their childhoods. Others have written stories from their growing up. All the documents have been put into a photocopied book and shared with the group. Some excerpts include:

> *In 1938 we had a hurricane. The whole family, two parents and seven kids stayed in the house to keep the wind from blowing the windows out and the house from blowing over.*

The streets had been closed to traffic to allow for sledding…we whizzed down the street in a dish pan or a piece of cardboard, this was the Depression. There were sleds, but only for the rich kids.

One 4th of July, we all had scarlet fever and were quarantined for a month or more. Pat O'Keefe (a local police officer) brought us fire works and a big watermelon, and put it on the porch for us. We were allowed to come out that night and set them off. He always had all the kids under his wing.

In those days girls kept to "girls play" and likewise the boys, except during the evenings. In summer we were allowed to play games like kick the can where the boys would excel and appear manly. Danger was our middle name. Reed Street was constructed on steep ledges that we thought were there to climb.

Gerry said, "Some people never gave the Reed Street Kids a fighting chance, but we all turned out real good, and the friendships we made on that street have stuck for life."

BLAZE OF GLORY

The year was 1937, and Clarence Fairchild, age twelve, was an adolescent boy with a little too much time on his hands. His mother had moved him and his brother Robert to Brattleboro to be closer to her sister Minnie when she left the boys' father in Bethel on the farm where her children had been born.

Divorce was not socially acceptable in the 1930s, and there were practical problems as well. Jenny, Clarence's mother, spent long hours working for the WPA, sewing pajamas for twenty-five cents per day. On the weekends she waited tables at the Hotel Billings Restaurant.

Each day she made lunch and sometimes dinner for her boys and then left for work. Clarence sold *Brattleboro Reformer*s in the afternoons on Main Street, but even with the list of chores his mother left for him each day, he found himself without much to do and no one to keep an eye on him and his activities during the summer.

The flaming airplane was thrown from the ledge of Reed Street, seen at the back of the photo. It hit the last building on the left and fell into the Whetstone Brook.

The Fairchild family lived on Reed Street where, like most families, they struggled to pay the rent and keep food on the table, but the neighborhood was full of good, hardworking folks. The Haus brothers were about Clarence's age. They had a great talent in their ability to create paper airplanes out of old newspapers. The three boys spent hours together producing gigantic, well-crafted airplanes, which they sometimes sent sailing off the slate ledges in front of Reed Street. (This was years before the Holstein Friesian was built.)

When they weren't making airplanes, they were reading comic books. One warm day, the boys were working on a masterpiece of an aircraft while one of them looked at the ads in the back of the comic book for fireworks. Suddenly, an exciting plan was hatched. They would save up enough money to order a big box of pyrotechnics, create a magnificent paper airplane, attach the explosives and launch it.

For months the boys pooled their pennies until the following summer, when they had saved enough money to order the gigantic package of illegal goods. When the parcel arrived, they loaded up the firecrackers and rockets onto the airplane and waited until traffic became congested when workers were traveling home by car and foot.

And that's how it came to pass that sometime in July 1938, three boys stood on top of the slate wall overlooking the park, lit a paper airplane loaded with explosives and commenced to send it flying into the air over the passing cars at malfunction junction.

As my father used to tell the story,

> *Everyone stopped at once and looked up to see this blazing ball of fire flying over Main Street. The firecrackers were popping and the rockets were commencing and there was smoke everywhere. About halfway between the park and the Whetstone Brook the thing blew up in a blaze of glory. Then it crashed right into the wall on the south side of Barrows Coal Company and fell into the brook. It was a beautiful sight. Absolutely unforgettable.*

As the eyes of the public watched the plane tumble down into the waters, their heads turned logically to follow the shouts of joy coming from the boys who were absolutely delighted that their plan, after eleven months of effort, had been perfectly executed.

But their pleasure was short-lived. Mr. Angus J. McKinnon, a local police officer, had also seen the sight. Yelling my father's name determinedly in his Irish brogue, he ran down the street and up South Main Street hill as fast as his middle-aged legs could carry him, while shouting "Fairchild! This is it! You're going up the river to Vergennes this time! It's reform school for you!"

But Mr. McKinnon never did find the boys, who were running, as my father told me, "as fast as any long skinny legs could carry three young fellows."

And despite numerous threats, he never was sent away to reform school either. As one former Reed Street resident told me many years later, "Mr. McKinnon always warned your father he was going to catch him, but did you notice that he never did? I'm not sure his heart was ever really in the chase."

ERNEST W. GIBSON JR., HOMETOWN HERO

On any given day, hundreds of people pass in front of the Gibson-Aiken Center, but not everyone is familiar with the lives of the two men for whom the building is named. Allow me to introduce Ernest W. Gibson Jr.

He was born in Brattleboro in 1901. He graduated from Brattleboro High School in 1919, from Norwich University in 1923 and from George Washington University Law School three years later. He was admitted to the Vermont Bar in 1926 and came home to Brattleboro to begin a law practice with Frank E. Barber.

Gibson was elected Windham County state's attorney and served from 1929 to 1933. He also served as secretary of the state senate until 1940. In June of that year, his father, U.S. senator Ernest Gibson, died. Then Governor George D. Aiken appointed his good friend and neighbor interim senator to complete his father's term until the special election of 1940 could be held.

Gibson did not run to keep his father's senatorial seat, having been called to war in the Pacific. Entering the service as a captain because he had served in the reserves, Gibson worked in the G-2 (intelligence) of the Forty-third Infantry Division and organized a divisional Japanese language intelligence section, which was a first in the Pacific Theater. In 1943, he found the famous green coconut with the message of rescue for the survivors of PT-109, written by John F. Kennedy.

Gibson spent a lot of his time at the front and was wounded by shrapnel from a bomb during an air raid. On Christmas Day 1945, he was discharged as a full army colonel, having earned the Legion of Merit, a Silver Star, Purple Heart and a War Department Citation.

Gibson returned to Brattleboro and reopened a law office with his brother Preston and A. Luke Crispe. An active lawyer, he was known to be determined to hold onto his own views but always tried to see the other side of the story.

In a 1972 interview, A. Luke Crispe remembered his friend and co-worker as a fair and optimistic public servant: "You always knew where he stood. He was inclined to be for the underdog. He took the side of the common man and he was always interested in people. Even after he was appointed a district judge in 1950, you could expect to see him on a Saturday morning on a Main Street corner waiting for someone to talk to."

Against tremendous odds, Gibson defeated the incumbent Governor Mortimer Proctor in 1946 on a platform of ousting power from big business.

Crispe recalled,

> *He was a practical politician. He had a lot of power because he had a lot of friends. With this power, while he was governor, he increased welfare,*

reorganized the state government, was responsible for a new state office building and created the Vermont State Police.

Anybody could go in the governor's office and talk with him. He felt this was the way it should be. He was one of the most politically liberal governors Vermont has ever had. The liberal Republicans became known as the Aiken-Gibson Wing of the Vermont Republican Party, but Ernest was the last member of this wing to be elected to the governorship.

Gibson resigned his governorship in 1950 after President Harry S. Truman appointed him a United States district judge. He served until November 1969, when he died of a cerebral hemorrhage at Brattleboro Memorial Hospital.

Crispe remembered,

There was a summer that we went golfing. I was wearing one of those straw hats men used to wear. Ernest bet me fifty cents that he could knock a golf ball off the hat and hit it out on the green. He's got the ball on my new hat, ready to swing at it, when all of a sudden he takes his club and smashes a hole until there is a gaping hole in the hat and the ball has fallen through to the ground. He laughed for a minute and handed me fifty cents because he'd won the bet. But he also paid for a new hat. That was Ernest. He had a terrific sense of humor, he got the most he could out of life and he always laughed.

JANICE WRIGHT BODOR—A LOCAL GIRL REMEMBERS HER CHILDHOOD IN BRATTLEBORO

I was born in 1925 in Brattleboro, the second child of Andrew Chapin Wright and May Evelyn Saderman Wright, daughter of Swedish immigrants. I had an older brother, Edward Chapin Wright, born in 1923. We lived in a three-story white clapboard house with an unfinished cellar below, built in 1910. There was a large detached barn, a separate hen house and a large vegetable garden…

We lived on the second floor of this two-family house, and my father's widowed mother—Emily Harriet Chapin Wright—lived on the first floor. We called her "Grammy," although my father referred to her as "The Old Lady."

My childhood would be called idyllic now. We lived in the country on a dirt road, Greenleaf Street, half a mile from the bus line. There were a few farm-type houses along the road.

Water was supplied by a stone-lined well, running by gravity to a concrete reservoir in the cellar with an electric pump, so water was available just by turning on the tap. In the beginning we had heated water in the "reservoir" at one end of the black iron kitchen stove that burned wood or coal, but a bit later we got hot water tanks in the kitchens and converted the iron stoves to burn kerosene.

Across the road and down through the woods ran the Whetstone Brook. We had a swimming hole, which we children called "Big Ledge." This was in the extensive pinewoods that prospered all about for miles.

I went to elementary school at the so-called Academy School in West Brattleboro. This was the very building that had housed the Glenwood Ladies Seminary where my mother had gone to school, years earlier. Girls then had boarded there, and once or twice I was sent to the top floor for some reason by one of my teachers, and saw the windowless cubicles where the girls had slept in earlier days.

High school, for me, began in 1938 at the Brattleboro High School. My parents thought it best for me to enroll in the Commercial Course, which would ensure a livelihood. We still were in the Great Depression, and my parents certainly did not have the funds to send me to college, nor did it occur to me to work my way through. I grew up knowing that college was not in my future.

Our high school was formed with a number of castes, the lowest being the General Course and the highest being College Prep, as it was called. Those in College Prep were the elite, and they associated only among themselves. Commercial was about midway in the caste system. Throughout the four years, I did very well in high school and was involuntarily put into College Prep English where I did very well.

Our teacher, Mr. Chaffey, kindly demanded a photographic memory among his students, and I would read the pages of literature that were assigned until I could see them mentally and could read them off mentally in a test. In my senior year, Mr. Chaffey made me a co-editor of the Dial, *the prize-winning magazine our high school put out.*

I was recommended by Mr. J. Wiggin, the school principal, for a part-time job as a stenographer and typist to the manager of the local Montgomery Ward.

I accepted the job although I never had worked and certainly didn't want to begin, but knew I had to. That meant that after school I'd go to the store on Main Street (where Brown & Roberts Hardware is now located) and work each afternoon until 5, also from 9 to 9 each Saturday for which I received $8 a week. Saturdays after work, I'd catch the 9 o'clock bus to West Brattleboro and walk up Greenleaf Street in the dark to our house.

At graduation from high school, I was a fourth Austine Prize winner, and my picture was in the newspaper…I was a speaker at our graduation ceremonies in June 1942 and spoke about World War II, and several from our class went off to war and their own deaths.

PEOPLE AND BUSINESSES PAST IN BRATTLEBORO

Wright's Grill

The north end of Putney Road is bustling. The roundabout spews traffic swiftly and effectively in four assorted directions. Fuel and fast food are abundant. But as late as the mid-1960s, Putney Road was lined with farms and open land. The west side, from Kipling Cinema to Black Mountain Square, was full of cows, pasture and a couple of big red barns.

Back in 1938, past the end of the town water line—on the east side of the road where the current Dunkin' Donuts is located—sat a charming restaurant with a small counter, two modest rooms and a total of eight booths. Wright's Grill became the most popular eatery in Brattleboro and stayed in business for over fourteen years. The eatery had such a fine reputation that people speak of it fondly some fifty years later. Locals came in for breakfast and homemade donuts. The folks from American Optical swung by for lunch. Families arrived for dinner. In between, the traveling salesmen, the tourists motoring up Route 5 and the teenagers looking for a place to enjoy an ice cream soda all came by to visit Wright's.

Owned by A. Chapin Wright and his wife May, Wright's was a family place open from 7:00 a.m. to 10:00 p.m. One might order all you could eat pancakes any time of day with real maple syrup for $0.35, fresh fried clams or scallops for $1.15 or enjoy the most expensive item on the menu, a club steak, for $2.50. Chape (as Mr. Wright was called by his friends) created a new local sensation, chicken fried steak: a small cube steak dipped in clam

Wright's Grill on Putney Road. *Courtesy of Cecilia S. Wright.*

batter and deep fried. He developed the idea himself after reading about a similar recipe in a magazine.

For dessert there was an unusual offering. "There was a sign on the wall that said 'Elephant's Delight,'" he remarked. "It was three scoops of ice cream with three different sauces in a glass dish for $0.35. I don't know how the dessert got its name, but when customers would ask what the sign meant, many people would smile and say, 'Three scoops! I couldn't eat that many!' Still, it was pretty popular." Cynthia worked as a waitress at the restaurant from the time she was thirteen. "People also enjoyed seeing the real German helmet and a shell casing that sat on the mantel over the fireplace. My father brought them home as souvenirs after serving in France during World War I."

Barbara Hewes was also a waitress at the restaurant in the late '40s. "Mr. Wright was a wonderful man to work for, and it was a great place to work as a teenager. We had a little gift shop that sold maple sugar and Vermont trinkets. The tips were good too. In those days, if you made twenty-five or fifty cents that was a lot of money."

Catherine Emond holds Wright's in her memory for a unique reason:

> *My husband and I were married on July 23, 1949, on a Saturday morning at St. Michaels Church on Walnut Street, and then everyone went*

> *to Wright's for a breakfast reception. Mr. Wright was so kind, everybody was so friendly. The place was like home. It was a wonderful way to celebrate a marriage and we all relaxed after the service. Mr. Wright closed the restaurant that morning just for us, but charged us practically nothing. It was really special.*

Wright's survived a fire in 1941, rationing in World War II, the sad death of May Wright and, later, the happy marriage of Mr. Wright to Cecilia Wood, the head waitress. There was heavy competition from the new Howard Johnson's down the road, Hill Home Inn on Putney Road and the Brattleboro Restaurant on Main Street, but Wright's was always at the top of its game. By 1952, Mr. and Mrs. Wright were exhausted by the long hours the restaurant required, and they sold the business. Years later, the building became Mort's Roadhouse, until it was torn down to make way for Dunkin' Donuts.

The next time you're whipping around the drive-thru, try to picture Putney Road as it once was. Time and traffic moved slowly and everyone had time for a cup of coffee at Wright's Grill.

Wendell Covey, Brattleboro's "Egg Man"

Wendell Covey sold his first dozen eggs in West Brattleboro, Vermont, when he was five years old. The year was 1919. He brought them to Frank LeRay's Grocery Store at 414 Western Avenue (located on the corner of Western Avenue and Greenleaf Street), and was paid a silver dollar for them. He's kept that silver piece to this day. Mr. Covey is ninety-eight now, but his feelings about his egg business have never changed.

> *I was always fascinated by laying hens and my mother showed me how to take care of them. I learned a lot in 4-H too.*
>
> *By the time I was fifteen I had my own egg business, delivering on my bicycle. I bought thirteen hens and a rooster from the Dunklee Farm. They were all free range out in the barnyard. My mother would help me out. She'd go down to the barn and pick up eggs twice a day and take them up to the house. When I got home, I would have to clean them and buff them and put them into boxes. Back in 1919 people sold eggs in a paper bag, but by then I had boxes to put them in.*

> *I got myself an old pickup truck when I was nineteen, painted it red and hand lettered the name of my business on the door. My business has always been called Covey's Chick A Biddy Farm, but everyone always called me the Egg Man.*
>
> *My first big customer was Mrs. Buchanan. She ran a boardinghouse on Terrace Street. I just kept growing from there, little bit by little bit over the years. The county agents would help me out too. People were always asking them where you could get nice fresh eggs in town. "Just call Mr. Covey," they'd say.*

Fast forward to 1974; Wendell was delivering eggs five days a week. He made eight hundred stops to homes, schools and stores, delivering 3,500 eggs per day, 24,500 per week. In his truck, eggs were packed in fifteen or thirty dozen cases. But he still sold by the dozen to homes all over Brattleboro.

When asked if there was always someone home to receive his delivery, Wendell laughs.

> *Oh no! Not everyone was home. I was showed where the key was and I walked right inside the house and put the eggs right in the refrigerator. I always said, "You ask any of the other ladies on my route. You can always trust your egg man."*
>
> *Many of the women on my route knew that I loved pecan pie, and come Christmastime there was often a piece of pie waiting for me in the refrigerator. One year I was given seven whole pecan pies and thirty boxes of chocolates!*

Tremendous growth took place at his farm too. The barn held cages for the eight thousand layers it took to fill all his orders. Baby chicks were arriving every three months. In 1968, a fully automated system was installed that washed, graded and boxed the eggs. The grain truck was pulling up to the barn with nine tons of grain every ten days. Regular trips had to be made to a specialty egg box maker in Massachusetts to bring back the eight thousand egg boxes needed to fill his orders every month. Wendell Covey's egg business was booming. Maple Farms, a local dairy operating on Putney Road, offered to buy him out.

"I said a polite no thank you. I had long days but I loved what I was doing. You have to love the public if you're going to make a go of it."

When asked which part of the business he loved the most, Mr. Covey becomes uncharacteristically shy.

I loved those birds. They were always number one. I treated them well. Nowadays they push the birds so much. The longer the daylight they have, the more grain they eat, the higher the protein they receive, the more eggs they produce. But I always believed that you have to do your job well. You treat the birds right and they treat you right. I'd pick up an egg and there was value there. I used to think, "There is a nickel in my pocket" when I went out to collect all those eggs.

The Hillside Dairy

Mr. John Sadd, a Brattleboro native, was wounded while serving his country in Germany from 1943 to 1945. When he came home to his wife Veronica and their children, he returned to his job as foreman in the framing department of H. Margolin & Co. Inc., a pocket book manufacturer located at the time on Vernon Road.

"My wife's family ran a big dairy farm in Whately, Massachusetts. It was called Hillside Dairy. They owned one in Greenfield too. When the Sinclair's Dairy on Washington Street came up for sale, my brother-in-law said, 'Why don't you get into the dairy business?'" Mr. Sadd remembers with a chuckle. "'That way the whole family will be in the milk business.' The dairy was in operation from 1946 to 1967."

When Sadd started Hillside, there were twenty small dairies in Brattleboro, many of which were tucked away in neighborhoods. Hillside Dairy was at 7 Washington Street and a competitor, Shaw Dairy, was located at 6 Myrtle Street. By the time they closed their doors in 1967, only two dairies were left in town, both located on Putney Road: Geo. E.Thomas & Son and Maple Farms.

Milk was purchased from six different local farmers and brought to Washington Street for processing.

We had our own milk cans, and we went to the farmers to pick up the milk in our pickup truck. From there we pasteurized it, homogenized it and so forth. We started our milk routes for delivery at three o'clock in the morning. We delivered seven days a week. After a while we couldn't find help that was willing to work seven days a week, so we went to four delivery days instead. We had between four hundred and five hundred customers, and drove out as far as Jacksonville, Vermont, to deliver. We also sold to schools and restaurants.

In those days, people bought their dairy products from one person instead of going to a grocery store. We sold our own milk, cottage cheese, ice cream and we also carried butter. A quart of milk was ten cents. We sold to a lot of families. They would order five to eight quarts of milk at a time. We would take our milk carriers loaded with milk right into their homes and put it in the refrigerator. They would line the empty bottles up alongside the refrigerator. We'd collect those and be on our way.

We also had milk boxes that people kept beside their doors that were insulated. When you deliver milk at three o'clock in the morning in the winter, it was a job to keep it from freezing. The boxes worked well for that. They also kept the milk cooler in the summer if we weren't bringing it right inside the house.

At that time we were selling milk in brown bottles. It was thought that the colored bottles helped to keep the sunlight out of the milk so that it didn't hurt the milk. Later on it was discovered that the color of the bottle didn't matter and we went to clear bottles.

We sold out of the dairy too. There was an ice cream stand. We made our own ice cream. We had all the regular flavors, vanilla, chocolate, strawberry, as well as butter pecan, banana temptation and orange pineapple, which were always favorites. A cone cost five cents. You could also buy a two-and-a-half-gallon container for about four dollars. We delivered ice cream too. At the peak of our production, counting the girls who worked the stand, we had about fourteen employees.

Mrs. Sadd worked at Hillside while raising the couple's five children. She says, "I helped with the bookkeeping. That was quite a job. It was a good way to raise a family though. Our kids always had plenty of milk to drink."

Eventually the style of how people bought their food began to change, bringing an end to the neighborhood dairies in town. Hillside was the last small dairy to go.

"When we finished, there were few people home during the day," Mr. Sadd commented. "That's why we closed. There were so many people who worked and they began to buy their milk at the grocery store on their way home. Times had changed over the years. People locked their doors. I can't say I blame them. I keep my door locked now too."

Sherwood Lake—The Sunbeam Bread Man

I came to Vermont from a New York state town with 350 people in it. When I got out of the army, where I served as a police officer, I wanted to get back into police work, but in 1958 jobs were hard to come by. That's when I became a bread delivery man.

Goddard Bakery was located in Claremont, New Hampshire, and Sunbeam was a trade name that was franchised out. They had ¾-ton trucks that were yellow with the Sunbeam girl painted on the side in the blue dress and pigtails. There were forty trucks that did house-to-house delivery, and wholesale to mom and pop stores. There were two bread routes running out of Brattleboro. Lyman Howe owned his own truck and the route running up the West River Valley.

I had the other route, which included all of Brattleboro, Putney, Dummerston, Westmoreland and into Richmond, New Hampshire. I delivered house to house and to small stores. The Newton family kept a small store in Dummerston Center; it was really a front room where they kept bread, milk, canned goods and staples. Ray LaPalme had a little store in West Dummerston, and there was another in which the post office was located. There were also small stores in every little village.

I bought the bakery products direct, kept track of all the customers. I had to pay tomorrow for what I sold today, and at the end of the week, Goddard made up the difference, which was my paycheck.

I bought bread for nineteen cents per loaf and sold it for twenty-three cents. King-sized loaves were purchased for twenty-three cents and sold for twenty-nine cents. We had Table Talk pies too. I bought them for fifty-one cents and sold them for fifty-nine cents. We sold Dolley Madison cakes. Donuts were fifty-nine cents a dozen. I also sold dinner rolls, white, wheat, Italian, rye and pumpernickel bread.

The bread that I didn't sell, I could sell back. They had a "stale store" in Claremont, and for a little while, one on Elliot Street where the Spic and Span laundry is now. If I was thinking I'd be selling a lot of pies during the week, and ordered, say one hundred, if I didn't sell those, I'd be stuck with them because Goddard didn't bake them themselves. For a while, my wife and I sold the leftovers from a small store we had at our apartment on Frost Street.

I had a sample basket. I would walk up to the door; the lady of the house would pick out what she wanted. When someone was a regular customer I went right in the house and put the bread in the freezer.

I found being a bread man like any job. It had its ups and downs. Summer was booming. There were summer camps, and I sold to the Hinsdale Raceway. There were also all the trailers out back where the people who owned the horses lived. They bought their bread from me.

But in the wintertime, sometimes there was hardly enough business to pay for the gas for the truck, and the going wasn't all that great. I got stuck in the snow and mud more than once.

There were five or six of us in competition. Bond Bread had four routes, Chuck Lavalla sold for Cushman Bread and Clayton Beliveau sold for Hathaway Bread. We shared information so that if one guy got stung we all knew. You could buy a lot of bakery products for five dollars, so when the bill got up around that point I asked folks to pay up. Most people were really good and there weren't many problems.

Retail routes gradually faded out as people started going to supermarkets. Goddard Bakery sold out in the fall of 1964. I went to work for Bond for four months, but I left because the handwriting was on the wall.

By July 3, 1965, I was done delivering bread, and on July 4, 1965, I went to work for the Brattleboro Police Department and stayed thirty years. I used to joke that I was the only guy in town who was thrown a parade to celebrate the day they started work.

THE ICE MEN

At the end of Frost Place, springs of water bubble with local history. Some believe this source to be the famous water that was pumped to Elliot Street for the "Brattleboro Water Cure" in the 1800s, which was located at the building currently housing the Brattleboro Fire Department. The Water Cure was used by a wealthy population.

But at the turn of the century, the springs became indispensable to everyday life in town. The introduction of iceboxes for home refrigeration about 1910 created a need for increased ice manufacturing. The famous springs became known as ice from Crystal Springs Ice Company.

Originally owned by the Whitney brothers, the company was first located on Linden Street. A 1914 ad in the *Brattleboro Reformer* offers an opportunity

Ice is cut by handsaw and hauled by horses on the Frost Street ice pond. Estey Buildings sit above on Birge Street.

to purchase ice in advance via coupon books sold at the company's office or at Simon's Specialty Shop on 107 Main Street. Prices were as follows: three-hundred-pound block, $1.00; five-hundred-pound block, $1.60; and one-thousand-pound block, $3.00. There was an "auto truck for hurry-up and long distance calls."

At that time, the springs were built into the form of two large ponds at the end of Frost Place. Ice was harvested by hand with the help of horses that pulled the three-hundred-pound blocks, which were stored on site in barns, heavily packed in sawdust.

By 1945, the Whitney brothers sold the business to Leon Whitman. By then the ice manufacturing process was mechanized using water from the springs. In a building forty by eighty feet long, huge tin cans were filled with the water. An overhead crane lifted the cans and placed them into a bath of brine. It took twenty-four hours to freeze the cans, which solidified from the outside in. The crane would then dip the cans into water, and when rocked by hand to encourage its release, a three-hundred-pound block of ice would slip out. The blocks were then scored so that the deliveryman would be able to chip off a twenty-five-, fifty-, seventy-five- or one-hundred-pound block.

Greg Whitman remembers delivering ice with his father and employee Robert Johnson.

> *It was the late 1940s, and it was exciting to go with my dad and Bob on the delivery route. We had regular customer routes in Brattleboro and vending machines that we needed to fill every day with ice cubes in Keene, New Hampshire, and Bellows Falls, Vermont.*
>
> *We'd back up to the loading docks and fill the truck with the huge blocks of ice. There was a big insulated blanket that went over the load. Sometimes we'd ice up railroad cars with literally a ton of ice. We'd drop the three-hundred-pound blocks through the top of the train. Sometimes we used crushed ice, especially for farmers to ice down their milk cans.*

Robert Johnson was an employee at Crystal Ice and Fuel (now known as CIFCO) for over forty years.

> *When I first started out, we had a combination truck with a tank on the front to deliver kerosene, and we had the ice in the back. There were yellow and black cards, which hung in the window of the residence. They had a big number on them indicating how many pounds of ice I was to deliver.*
>
> *I wore a rubber apron. I slipped it on over my arms, and it covered my back so that as I carried the ice, I didn't get wet when it dripped. I would go to the back of the truck, chip at the block to make it the right size, grab the ice with my tongs and throw it over my back to bring it inside the house. It could be a long trip up a third-floor walk up, but I was in good shape from the work.*
>
> *I always left the ice chips on the back of the truck for the kids. It was pretty special for them, like having Popsicles.*

Greg Whitman remembers when the ice business dried up. "Over the years the need for ice changed. First came rural electrification, people bought electric refrigerators. Then, by the 1970s with high-energy costs and less demand for ice, we decided to stop manufacturing it. Ice was kind of like the buggy whip. It just was not needed anymore."

Arlene Georgina, Fifty Years of Beauty

Arlene Searles Georgina was in Brattleboro High School in 1954 when one of her friends told her she was going to go to Houle's Beauty Academy in Manchester, New Hampshire, and asked if Arlene would have any interest in joining her.

"I would just love to," replied Arlene, "but I don't know if I'll be able to get the money together." "Wouldn't you know it?" she chuckles now, "I went to school and she didn't."

Fifty years later, Georgina still loves the job that she chose for herself when she was only seventeen.

> *I love the people and the conversation. I like to see how people look when they come in, and how they feel when they go out. For me, it's all about the transformation.*
>
> *I started out in 1956 at Nina's Beauty Shop, located over where the Food Co-op is today. I only worked on the days she called me in and was paid five dollars for a day's work. One day Ludwig Gunzinger asked me to come into his shop and do a finger wave on a model. Those are very tough to do. If I did it right the first time, he promised to employ me. I was hired for forty dollars a week and stayed twelve years.*

Gunzinger was known for strolling about town in a fur coat with a shoulder bag.

> *He was quite a character. One day I asked him why he did it, and he said it was the best advertising. People would point to him and say "That's Ludi Gundzinger. He owns the beauty shop on Elliot Street."*
>
> *I opened my own shop, Arlene's Beauty Salon, in 1969* [and ran it] *for the next 22 years. At that time a shampoo and set went for $2.75. Can you believe that?*
>
> *In beauty school we had to take an anatomy class. I felt like I was in nursing school. We had to know the human body from the waist up. We were told that we'd need this knowledge because we would be holding human heads in our hands while we shampooed them.*
>
> *Techniques have really changed over the years. I had to learn how to give a machine perm. Those were big machines and it cost about ten dollars to get your hair curled. That was big money in the 1930s and '40s when*

they were most popular. I never had to use one, since the technology changed around 1959, but one customer came in and told me that she had heard about a fire in a Boston salon. When the fire broke out everybody ran, and the woman who was hooked up to one of those permanent wave machines burned because she couldn't get unhooked.

Lots of things have changed over the years. Coloring hair used to be pretty simple. Now it is a real science. And, in the early days, women used to come to the beauty parlor once a week. Now they come every six weeks or every few months.

The first half an hour is usually the shampoo and set. Then it's all about the visiting. People love to come and tell me their stories, and I look forward to seeing each customer. My clients like the chance to sit and talk about their lives. We girls used to joke that when we went to get our license that we should ask for a psychiatrist license too. We do a lot of listening to people's troubles, but we don't get paid like they do!

These days, Arlene can be found at Scissor Masters on Elliot Street. "I have several clients who have been with me way back to the '50s. Some of them can't get to me, so I go to their homes and bring them in. I could probably do their hair for them at home, but I think it's good for older people to get out. I don't expect a tip for doing that. I do it because I think it's the right thing to do."

DOING A LITTLE TRADING IN BRATTLEBORO

When my grandfather Fairchild needed a few groceries, he would ask me to "drive Downstreet to do a little trading." This turn of phrase dated back to his days as a farmer in Bethel when he would literally bring farm goods into the local store to exchange for dry goods.

At the beginning of the twentieth century, general stores kept goods behind the counter. A clerk found each item for the shopper. In 1916, the self-service grocery store idea was patented. No longer did a clerk need to wait on customers; instead, the customer waited on himself or herself.

In Brattleboro, grocery and specialty stores were scattered all over town. The Public Market, founded by the Broutsas family and then purchased by the Briggs brothers, Russell and Neil, was an upscale store that carried higher grades of meat and S.S. Pierce products. Through the '60s, one

The Public Market on lower Main Street, founded by the Broutsas family. *Courtesy of Constantine "Dicko" Broutsas.*

could purchase escargot from France and Danish marzipan. Its main competition was Fisher's Market, where the Sevca store was recently located on Elliot Street.

There were too many stores to name here, but some included Bickford's Store at 407 Western Avenue, which was actually a home with the store in the living room portion; Bushnell's IGA at 94 Elliot Street, which was torn down when the parking garage was built; Centerville Grocery located at the top of Williams Street; and Clark Avenue Grocery, where a computer store is now housed.

Main Street held the major grocery stores. The First National Grocery Store was located where the Underground now stands. The hardwood floors were regularly polished and washed. They creaked as customers pushed their wire buggies about the store.

The Grand Union was tucked into the back of what is now the parking lot on High Street.

The Great Atlantic and Pacific Tea Company, otherwise known as the A&P, was located where the Key Bank is now located. The coffee grinder near the front of the store allowed the aroma of fresh coffee to permeate the air.

In the days before electric conveyer belts, A&P customers placed their groceries on a metal surface at check out. Three pieces of wood, two long side pieces and one to hold the groceries at the back, connected to a large metal handle. As the clerk slid the items over to the person bagging the groceries, he would pull the metal handle to push more groceries toward him, which took considerable strength. The shopper would then place more groceries at the back of the slide. This process required some coordination and cooperation between the clerk, the shopper and their small children, as fingers could easily become pinched in the process.

Good shopping etiquette also required that the customer find the sticker price of each item and place it such that the clerk could easily find the price and punch the numbers into the manual cash register.

As shoppers continued to press stores for more items, the downtown grocery stores began to rebuild and expand to areas on the outskirts of town.

First National built a new store on Canal Street where the Price Chopper is now located. Considerably smaller than the current store, First National was a swanky place. It featured floor-to-ceiling glass windows in the front of the store and a cleaver grocery pickup system.

After filling two paper bags, the bagger placed the food into a sturdy metal box with a number painted on the outside. The customer was given a piece of cardboard reflecting the number on the box. The bagger then turned toward the front of the store and placed the metal box on the rollers, which went the length of the front of the store.

As the groceries loudly moved and approached the end of the line, a magical sensor opened a small glass door, which sent the box around a corner to the outside of the store. There, a bagboy waited.

After the customers paid for her groceries, she would pull her car to the front of the store, pop the trunk and give the help her cardboard number. He would load each bag of groceries into the car.

In the late 1970s, grocery stores moved to warehouse style, meaning the end of an era. Yet when I make my weekly run to the Brattleboro Food Co-op, where the P&C once stood, I still tell the kids, "I'm off to do a little trading."

THE ERA OF THE SECOND WORLD WAR

A War Ends, Brattleboro Celebrates

Then twenty-year-old Greenleaf Street resident Janice Wright Bodor, who served as Brattleboro assistant town clerk, documented her experience of V-J Day.

> *This evening, about six-thirty, a news commentator stated that he expected there would be an important announcement. There have been innumerable expectations of important announcements but this seemed more urgent and we thought it might really be the end of the war.*
>
> *At seven o'clock I went downstairs where my grandmother was listening to the radio and sure enough, about thirty seconds after seven o'clock, another commentator relayed to us the president's proclamation that the Japanese had accepted our surrender terms!*
>
> *Down in the valley the air raid whistle was blowing one continuous blast and farther away toward town, some factory whistle was blowing continuously. During the last two or three weeks I have heard stories by old-timers tell of how they celebrated the Armistice in 1918. After we had some sherry and crackers, I began to feel more pepped up and curious about what was going on in town.*
>
> *I rushed upstairs, changed my clothes and grabbed Cynthia* [her younger sister] *and my grandmother, and I drove Downstreet. This was only about fifteen minutes after the declaration but the streets were jammed with lines and lines of horn-blowing cars with screaming occupants.*

Residents gather on the corner of Main and High Streets as news of victory spreads. Notice the decorated cars on the far right. *Courtesy of the family of Jenny Russell.*

We joined in and edged our way in the car up and down Main Street four times, madly blowing the horn, almost deaf from the din of the crowds. Then we got out of traffic and drove up on Putney Road to the restaurant [where Dunkin' Donuts is currently located] *to get my father.*

He closed up to let the waitresses celebrate and we went back through the streets again. On the way up to get him we would pass an occasional car rushing to Brattleboro, and I'd blow a victory salute on the horn and usually they'd blast back.

We went back home to pick up Mother, who hadn't come the first time, then back to Brattleboro and stayed until about eleven o'clock, watching the procession of cars, all with people clogging the running boards, bumpers and even riding on the roofs, all yelling and beating syrup cans and throwing confetti and serpentine and toilet paper, roll after roll. The cars would go to one end of Main Street and then turn around and go to the other end with people continually jumping on cars and then off and then on to some other.

The streets were thick with layers of paper scraps and brilliant confetti. There was high cloudiness Tuesday night and about nine o'clock a gusty wind sprang up, which whipped the confetti into swirls.

We went back to the restaurant and when we got into the comparative blackness of Putney Road we could see the shifting clouds and how once in a while the moon would glow through a thin layer of clouds. There were cars with steam whistles tied to their exhaust pipes so they'd screech when the motor was raced, cars dragged cans and wash tubs and rusty shovels; people carried red and green flares; some boys carried flaming brooms; an impromptu parade started gathering people as it went; one car had the head of a store-window mannequin stuck on its radiator cap; another car had a wooden American eagle propped up on its hood; one car had a big American flag streaming from its staff, which was tied to the front bumper; there were big trucks with the back ends so jammed with yelling people I don't see how they breathed. I bet there was more than one case of sagging running boards the next day!

Everyone was everybody's friend—one girl passing in a car yelled to me "Hi Blondie," a man in Legion uniform grabbed my arm as he passed riding on another car, everybody waved at everybody who waved at them and yelled back and forth.

Veteran's Village

Brattleboro native Margaret Whitney, then fifteen years old, was working the soda fountain at the Latchis Food Store on the corner of Elliot and Main Streets in 1942 when Hinsdale, New Hampshire native Tom O'Connell, then sixteen, came into the store for a hot fudge sundae. They were married four years later.

O'Connell enlisted in the army when he turned eighteen and was shipped to Germany during World War II. He came back to the States when the war ended and reenlisted in the service, thinking at first that he would make the army a career. He was stationed at Fort Mead in Maryland.

Margaret and Tom took out a marriage license on three different occasions, but the army moved Tom so many times that each license expired. Finally, on January 4, 1947, Margaret took the train from Brattleboro to Baltimore. They got a fourth marriage license in Annapolis, walked to the minister's house and knocked on the door. The minister told the young couple that his wife wasn't feeling well, and that if they would wait until he fed his kids dinner, he'd be happy to marry them.

"He told us that we were going to have a real church wedding," recalls Margaret, "and he walked us down the street to a beautiful cathedral. We had the wedding in that gorgeous church, just the three of us."

When Tom was discharged from the service, they came home to Brattleboro.

"There were no apartments to be had. All the local housing was full. We had a child and nowhere to live," said Margaret.

Thousands of young men were drafted or enlisted into the armed services between 1940 and 1945. A majority of them had lived with their parents prior to World War II. Years later, the war won, they had become veterans, and many married and began having families of their own. A housing shortage ensued nationwide.

One of Brattleboro's answers to the problem was creating approximately fifty houses on the land now occupied by the Little League Field on the corner of Moreland Avenue and South Main Street. The area had held only a sandbank before the houses were hastily built. The buildings, which came from Fort Devens in Massachusetts, were quickly dubbed Veteran's Village.

These prefabricated residences were two-family homes, each with its own tiny bedroom, bathroom and one small room that tripled as kitchen, living room and dining room. A kerosene cookstove graced the kitchen, and a portable oil burner heated each unit.

Margaret O'Connell remembers,

> *They were tiny places. Every inch of wall space had a piece of furniture on it. When the alarm clock went off, you could hear it all over the house and next door. We had a crib and our bed in the bedroom, and had to put the dresser in the living room because there wasn't enough room for it.*
>
> *All the houses were all the same, made of plaster board and were prefabricated so they went up fast. They cost twenty-seven dollars a month to rent, and that included electricity. There was heat, but no insulation. It was so cold the blankets would freeze to the walls.*

Mildred and Frank Timney of Vernon lived in Vet's Village for over four years. Mildred recalled,

> *Frank worked at Margolin's, the pocket book factory on Canal Street* [now the site of the Outlet Center] *where he was a cutter. We have four children now, but at the time we had one child who was under a year old. The neighborhood had lots of mothers walking lots of babies. Many of us*

didn't have cars and had to walk downtown with our children to the First National grocery store on Main Street. We walked everywhere. You got to know your neighbors because the walls were pretty thin.

About 1950, some of the houses were sold, and others were bulldozed to make way for the Little League field.

"No one lived there any longer than they had to," O'Connell said, "but we were grateful for Vet's Village. We had certainly lived in worse places. It served us well for the time that we needed it."

Business Briefs from 1946

Harmony Place Closed to Public
Parking Area Fenced Off, Do Not Enter Signs to Go Up
Entrance to Be Via Hotel Arch

A fence was erected in a new location on the private way between Elliot and High Streets in back of the Hildreth plant Monday and The Phoenix was told that "no parking" obstructions and "do not enter here" signs would mark the Elliot Street entrance, known as Harmony Place, shortly. The object, would be to avoid congestion cased by general public use of the private areas and two way traffic, and an effort is being made to carry out the experiment so that the situation will be as satisfactory as possible for those who have occasion to use the private way. The new fence is designed to keep the public out of the area in back of the Grange block.

"Do not enter here" signs on the Elliot Street end, if observed, would force cars and trucks entering the area to come through the Hotel Brooks arch from High Street, and through the hotel's parking area. The fence separating the hotel and Hildreth areas was removed last week by permission of the hotel in order to conduct the experiment.

The High-Elliot Street thoroughfare is not intended to be used by the general public, either for parking or for through travel, it was emphasized, but only by the property owners, tenants and their customers. Until the recent changes, helter-skelter parking, snow and trucks have made the narrower parts of the private way on the Elliot Street end congested and hard to traverse. Another suggestion urged Monday as a means of providing more parking space for the public was the opening up of private property behind tax-exempt First Baptist Church, Masonic Temple and library building, which along with their right of way in back of the post office and the parking area east of the Manley apartments would continue the proposed "back street" between Elliot and High Streets along up to Grove Street. Many cars could be parked in that section, it was observed. The Baptist property has recently been developed as a recreational area, with outdoor fireplace, swings and chutes for youngsters.

Legion Discusses Purchase of Home
Fred Harris Present to Talk About Bradley Property

Discussion of the possibilities of purchasing a new American Legion home by Brattleboro post took place at a meeting attended by over 75 members at the Legion rooms in the Community building Friday evening.

Fred H Harris, owner of the former Richard M. Bradley house on Putney Road, one of the three under consideration, was present to answer questions. He set no price, however, and advised the committee to inspect the property. The other properties suggested were the so-called Old Tavern, at 9 Canal Street and the DeAngelis apartment house at 92 High Street.

Building Sold at Elliot and Main
Mr. and Mrs. Apostoles Purchase Block from Bank

The three-story brick business block on the south corner of Elliot and Main Streets has been purchased from Vermont Savings Bank by Mr. and Mrs. Peter G. Apostoles. The block has two stores on street level, occupied by Lunden & Adams and J.F. Austin, offices on the second floor, and the Red Men's hall occupies part of the top story. Nicholas Bardis, who formerly was a partner of Apostoles in a restaurant business, purchased an adjacent block on Elliot Street only a few months previously.

Adams, Stuarts Buy Pine Heights
Boston Couple to Live at Former Fuller Estate

Walter N. Adams has purchased Pine Heights, an estate bounded by Pine and Canal Streets and Oak Grove Avenue, from the Abbie E. Fuller estate. Adams of this town and Florence and Earl Stuart of Boston who are planning to make their home in Brattleboro.

Adams said that when it is possible to undertake extensive remodeling the new owners plan to convert the mansion like dwelling into apartments. Some of the building lots will be offered for sale, he added.

Dunham Brothers Buys Hotel Garage
Acquires High St. Building from Brooks as Investment

Thursday Dunham Bros. Company completed arrangements for purchasing from the Hotel Brooks Inc., the building on High Street occupied by M&L Garage, Cummer Company and others.

Dunham Brothers Company as an investment is purchasing this and for the present no changes are contemplated.

Main Street, Brattleboro, 1950.

BRATTLEBORO IN THE 1950s

The First Winter Carnival

Thirty-two candidates vied for queen at the First Annual Brattleboro Winter Carnival held in 1957. Thirteen of the youthful contestants were unmarried, and nineteen of the contenders carried the word "Mrs." in front of their name. It was another time in American life.

The program for the first Carnival carried a message from Raphael U. Corbeil, chairman of the Queen Committee. It read, "Who will be the Queen? We will know at the Coronation. The spotlight will be on each one of you. You have all shown qualifications to be a Queen…from Brattleboro, The All-America City."

The program also featured a welcome from Fred H. Harris entitled "Why a Winter Carnival?" He wrote,

> *The gay and happy occasions now known as Winter Carnivals had their beginnings up north in Canada over fifty years ago…Carnival emphasizes healthful, outdoor exercise under blue skies and in keen, invigorating air when Nature is at its best. It is a time of colorful costumes, gala decorations, camaraderie and friendly feeling.*
>
> *…Carnival is a time for house parties. Instead of inviting friends to witness just one event like the Ski Jumping Tournament, why not invite them for a long week-end to see the various activities our progressive community has to offer?*

Compliments of
ALL STATES CAFE
"Where We Meet to Eat"
43 Main St.

Slalom Ski Wear
Duo Fold Ski Underwear
J. F. AUSTIN
Elliot St.

Open Letter to the Queen Contestants

By RAPHAEL U. CORBEIL
Chairman of Queen Committee

Who Will Be The Queen? We will know at the Coronation. The spotlight will be on each one of you. You have all shown qualifications to be a Queen, the Winter Carnival's Ambassador to Bermuda from Brattleboro, The All-America City.

The Queen Committee sincerely gives its heartfelt thanks to the Queen Candidates who have helped to make the 1957 Winter Carnival a success.

To the Queen, we extend our best wishes for a happy and successful reign.

Shown in the photograph: Thirty of the 32 candidates for Winter Carnival Queen make this pretty picture. Front row: Mrs. Ora L. Morrisseau, Mrs. Charlotte S. Abel, Miss Eleanor M. Jones; second row: Miss Mary E. Godfrey, Miss Dorothy A. Welcome, Miss Jayne Sparks; third row: Mrs. Dorothy Clark, Miss Judith A. Martin, Miss Evelyn Edson; fourth row: Mrs. Susan H. Barre, Mrs. Betty Ann Tyler, Miss Jane Robinson; fifth row: Mrs. Janet H. Reed, Mrs. Barbara E. Johnson, Miss Sylvia Mae Quinn; sixth row: Mrs. Marguerite P. Pierce, Miss Nancy Madden, Mrs. Eric Scott; seventh row: Mrs. Dorothy R. Austin, Miss Linda Mills, Mrs. Muriel N. Merrell; eighth row: Mrs. Shirley Vittum, Miss Gerry Shippee, Miss Martha Gould; ninth row: Mrs. Gerry Welch, Mrs. Marylin B. Orne, Mrs. Marie Germly; tenth row: Miss Joan Hewitt, Mrs. Phyllis Baldwin, Mrs. Ann Kempf. Miss Mary Jasienowski and Miss Christine Angell, not shown, were at play rehearsal at the Little Theatre.

Compliments of
LEVASSEUR'S GARAGE
INCORPORATED
406 Western Avenue

Compliments of
Angell's Automotive Service Inc.
Engine Rebuilding
Elliot St. Brattleboro

15

Program from the first Winter Carnival, February 1957.

The first Winter Carnival was a glorious three-day event that kicked off at 2:00 p.m. on Friday afternoon for the "Parade of the Queens." Queen candidates perched on floats accompanied by marching bands and champion baton twirlers.

Thirty youth groups displayed their artistry snow sculpturing on the Common in the afternoon. That evening a semiformal event took place at what was called the Community Building and is now referred to as the Gibson-Aiken Center. For the cost of a $1.50 ticket, couples could participate in the "highlight of the winter social season," dancing to local musician Dick Perry's Orchestra. The event was co-sponsored by the Brattleboro Outing Club and the Woman's Evening Club.

At 11:30 p.m., Master of Ceremonies Jerry Kearney interviewed the top five finalists of the "popularity contest" and selected the queen on the "basis of poise, personality and appearance." Then Lieutenant Governor Robert Stafford crowned Miss Eleanor "Twinkle" Jones.

Saturday featured competitive skiing and skating and an "Outdoor Evening" with "torchlight skiing and brilliant aerial fireworks." A square dance, which again featured Dick Perry's Band, was also held. On Sunday came "the thrilling climax to the Carnival weekend," the thirty- fifth annual ski jump on Harris Hill.

In an article in the program by Hal March Jr., the Ski Jump is referred to as "The Big Show." He writes, "During the last twenty-five years skiing has become the feature attraction in the carnival called winter. And ski jumping is its high wire act."

The names of the participants that year were not listed in the general program, but local jumpers Frank Barber, Phil Dunham, Richard "Tink" Austin and Merrill Barber are mentioned in other writings and pictures.

The program of events was sponsored by many local groups and businesses. The back cover features the Latchis Hotel. "Latchis Hotel is one of the very few Modern Hotels in New England," the ad reads. "It is equipped with the finest beds…the building of fireproof steel and concrete construction and every room with private bath and telephone."

Smaller ads featured Red Circle Auto Supply, Ted Sugar Furniture Store at 12 Main Street and Bushell's, "complete food Store and freezer locker," at 94 Elliot Street. Some businesses simply printed their names and assumed the reader knew where to find them. They included Tom Thumb Snack Shop, Frances Stores, Estey Organ Co, Turner's Flying "A" Service Station, Royal Diner, Brattleboro TV, H. Margolin & Co. and Goodnow Pearson & Hunt.

Other stores printed small tag lines with their ads. "Hungry?—Eat, Tired?—Sleep, Relax?—Bowl at Kings Drive In & Bowling Center." This establishment could be reached at Alpine 4-4591. Another ad reads, "First in Quality, fairest in prices, fastest in service, Ratti's Motor Mart."

Victor Harrison, sports editor at the *Daily Reformer*, summed up the tone of the weekend in his article "Brattleboro Winter Playland": "King Winter is still as rough and as unpredictable as ever but now his force has been turned to the benefit of the area and has made Brattleboro a complete winter playground."

How Living Memorial Park Was Born

It's easy to drive past Living Memorial Park on Guilford Street and take for granted its existence, but its beginnings involved almost every town resident.

Sixty-four years ago, William H. Evans of Townshend wrote a letter to the *Brattleboro Reformer*. He suggested that the people of Brattleboro create a fund by purchasing war bonds "equal to the number of Brattleboro men and women in the armed services," and that when the bonds matured, the money be used to provide a "living memorial." The Kiwanis Club liked the idea and the group became the sponsoring organization to begin the fund.

Those purchasing the bonds gave in honor of those serving in the armed services. But while the original suggestion was to dedicate a memorial to those in the service, it soon became clear that many people, not just those in the military, performed services worthy of recognition.

It was therefore decided that the park should be a living memorial to all. World War II was not yet over when the idea was launched and there were strong feelings that the park should be "dedicated to all those who love life and living and are worthwhile members of our free society," according to a document written by the Kiwanis Club at the time.

The bond drive was a huge success. With the bonds put into safekeeping until they matured, eventually $33,875 was raised.

The land upon which the park was built belonged to the estate of Minnie Clark, who had listed her farm for sale with a price tag of $35,000. But as the Clark family learned of the plans for the park, as their donation toward the project, they gave the difference between their asking price and the amount of money the town had to spend, a single donation of $1,125, a generous sum at the time.

With the park grounds now acquired, the land was turned over to the Town of Brattleboro under the guidance of the Recreation Board. There were countless people who served to guide the planning of the park, but some of the key players were Ellwood Allen, the original long-range planner; John Penney; John Malloy; Nelson Withington; Mrs. A.O. Brungardt; Malcolm McMaster; Helen Harris; and then town manager George Miller.

During 1955–56, the park grew faster than at any other equivalent length of time. Though it began under the guidance of Robert Billings, Elliot Barber, Floyd Messenger and John Dunham as the "Guilford Street Ski Tow" in 1937, the Rotary Club raised the funds to get the tow upgraded by 1955. Also in 1955, the Brattleboro Lions Club raised funds to build the road that leads to the upper level of the park.

A $3,000 contribution from Mr. and Mrs. Howard Rice allowed for the swampy area at the east end of the park to be worked so that the swimming pool could be located there. The Brattleboro Exchange Club loaned its services during the second year of work to drain the low and wet spots, making usable land out of the swamp and marshland.

While all of this activity was taking place, the Future Farmers of America, the 4-H Club and the area Boy Scouts worked on clearing the land and planting trees in other areas.

In early 1956, a major project was undertaken. In January of that year, a special town meeting authorized a bond issue for $115,000 to build the swimming pool. The vote passed by a margin of 1,232 to 181.

Meanwhile, the Brattleboro Elks Club worked on landscaping the area around the pool, the Kiwanis Club worked on the third level, building what became the covered picnic grounds, and the American Legion busied itself creating the softball diamond. Its auxiliary provided the money for the backstop.

On the second level, Dunham Brothers teamed with the Brattleboro Athletic Club to create a secondary field that was used for the Small Fry League before that field was moved to South Main Street.

In 1956, Brattleboro was entered in a nationwide contest for the All-American City award on the strength of what had been accomplished at the park. The town was one of twenty-two communities considered and won the competition.

The skating rink was added in the 1970s.

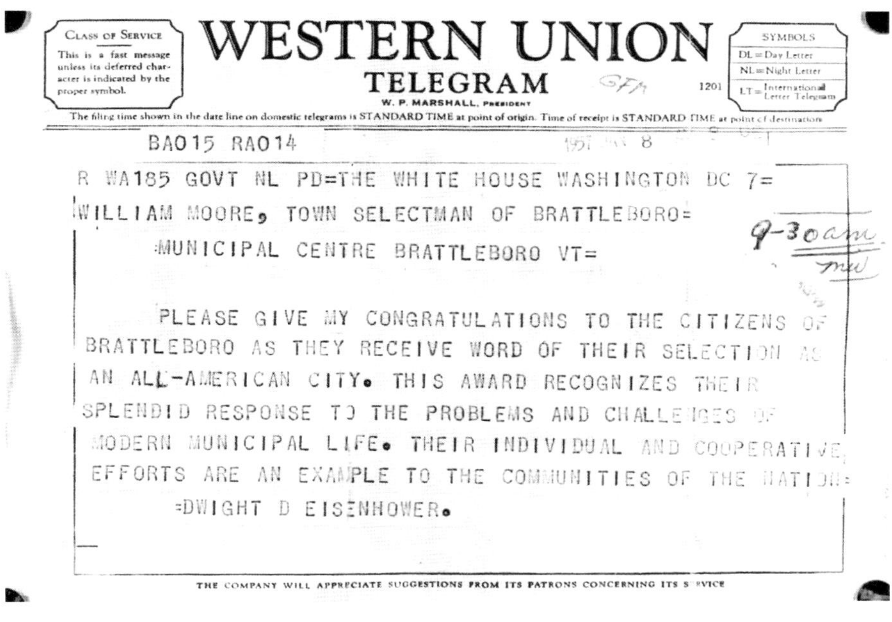

CLASS OF SERVICE
This is a fast message unless its deferred character is indicated by the proper symbol.

WESTERN UNION
TELEGRAM
W. P. MARSHALL, PRESIDENT

SYMBOLS
DL = Day Letter
NL = Night Letter
LT = International Letter Telegram

1201

The filing time shown in the date line on domestic telegrams is STANDARD TIME at point of origin. Time of receipt is STANDARD TIME at point of destination

BA015 RA014

R WA185 GOVT NL PD=THE WHITE HOUSE WASHINGTON DC 7=

WILLIAM MOORE, TOWN SELECTMAN OF BRATTLEBORO=

MUNICIPAL CENTRE BRATTLEBORO VT=

9-30 am

PLEASE GIVE MY CONGRATULATIONS TO THE CITIZENS OF BRATTLEBORO AS THEY RECEIVE WORD OF THEIR SELECTION AS AN ALL-AMERICAN CITY. THIS AWARD RECOGNIZES THEIR SPLENDID RESPONSE TO THE PROBLEMS AND CHALLENGES OF MODERN MUNICIPAL LIFE. THEIR INDIVIDUAL AND COOPERATIVE EFFORTS ARE AN EXAMPLE TO THE COMMUNITIES OF THE NATION=

=DWIGHT D EISENHOWER.

THE COMPANY WILL APPRECIATE SUGGESTIONS FROM ITS PATRONS CONCERNING ITS SERVICE

A telegram arrived from the White House at the office of the Brattleboro selectman, congratulating the town, from President Dwight D. Eisenhower.

FRANK DEARBORN: A LEGACY OF SERVICE AND A SMILE

"The greatest satisfaction for me is to have been able to work at a job I enjoy and to be motivated enough to see that the programs and services grow," said Frank Dearborn, Brattleboro's recreation director from 1957 to 1990, at the time of his retirement. "And that couldn't have happened without great community support."

It is Brattleboro's community that lured Dearborn to come in the first place. He arrived in 1957 from Fairport, New York, where he had been the recreation director, and from Mystic, Connecticut, prior to that.

"I was excited to come here and work in a community that was developing a park such as Memorial Park," he said.

Dearborn was pleased that taxpayers supported recreation and had acquired the fifty-three acres in 1955 to create Living Memorial Park. In fact, he is proud that he was able to achieve all of the original aims of the park plans, which included a ski tow, a swimming pool, two softball fields, an indoor ice-skating rink, tennis courts, a playground, a ski jump and a picnic area.

Another important addition to the recreation of Brattleboro was the purchase of the Gibson-Aiken Center in 1976. Prior to its purchase, the building was the local armory and the Recreation Department was stuffed onto the third floor. When the building was purchased, indoor activities like gymnastics and basketball grew, while the seniors enjoyed the space on the bottom floor.

Then Brattleboro town manager Corwin "Corky" Elwell said at the time of his retirement, "He's maintained the park's integrity through the years when it wasn't always easy to do. Frank is a very creative guy, but with a lot of practical sense. More than anything else he has a touch with people…and because of that he's been able to make the progress he has over the years."

But even more important than programs and buildings, Dearborn built relationships with members of the community through the years.

Sandy Ware, currently serving as the activities director at the Thompson House, remembers when Dearborn hired her to work the summer playground recreation program in the early 1960s: "I was a thirteen-year-old kid and he gave me my first job. I came back every summer to work for him all through college. He taught me so much, and Frank Dearborn is the reason why I became an activities director. He remains an inspiration to so many people."

I remember Mr. Dearborn and his station wagon appearing every year at the annual Easter egg hunt in the spring. Hundreds of eggs were hidden on the upper field at the park, along with the grand prize, the golden egg, which held a season's pass to the pool. Children were lined up on the grass, and when he yelled "Go!" they ran to pick up the candy eggs and hunt for the coveted golden one.

Each year I was stunned by the number of kids and became too overwhelmed to find a single candy egg. The kids moved like a vacuum cleaner over the field, and in minutes, the eggs were gone.

Mr. Dearborn would call for the small number of kids who didn't find any eggs, take them over to his station wagon and give each of us a smile and a few pieces of candy. He maintained that next year things might be different and encouraged us all to keep trying and to come back next year.

Dearborn's eldest daughter Donna isn't surprised. "My dad is the kindest, most compassionate man I've ever known. He cares about everyone."

When he retired in 1990, Dearborn fashioned his retirement around the fulfilling activities he loved, especially his favorite lifetime sports of hiking, biking, tennis, cross-country skiing and snow shoeing. It is no surprise that he was snow shoeing with his family one cold December day in 2003. What is shocking is that this prominent role model for health and fitness fell over and suffered an unexpected, debilitating stroke at the age seventy-five.

Donna remarks, "My dad has required complete care at Vernon Green Nursing Home for the last four years. We shower him with love and our presence. We do our best to carry on his legacy by living life as he showed us—with amazing patience, adventurous spirit and an unwavering positive attitude."

Skating and Some Thin Ice

"I'd say that on a Sunday afternoon or a nice evening, there were probably fifty people out on the ice," remembers Etta Simonds Mattison.

> *I lived in the neighborhood of what was then called Crystal Springs Ice, Wood & Trucking Co. (at Cross Place) down on Frost Street, so we were lucky enough to have skiing, sledding and especially ice skating right in our own backyard. That was in the mid- to late 1930s.*

Skating on the Connecticut River between the Brattleboro and Hinsdale, New Hampshire iron bridges.

> *The back pond wasn't used, they no longer cut ice out of it, and it was spring fed so it kept flooded. There was a floodlight out there and a little warming hut, it was awfully nice of Crystal Springs to provide that for the community. People came from all over town to skate there, but Robert "Punky" Deyo and his brother Tommy, and Neil and Beverly Crown and Katherine O'Donnell and I were lucky because we lived in the neighborhood and could run down the street and enjoy the ice.*
>
> *A girl named Shirley Lamoureaux lived up on Forest Street. She was quite a sight to see because she wanted to be a professional skater. She was so good!*

Prior to the building of the skating rink at Living Memorial Park in the mid-1970s, local people had their favorite spots to ice skate around town. There was an area out in back of the old high school, which is now the Municipal Center. Mr. Joseph Wiggin, the principal, was known to send the boys from detention out to shovel the ice as punishment.

The Crowell Lot on Western Avenue was usually flooded; the old Academy School had a skating pond in the 1940s as well, and there were the Retreat Meadows.

Maddie Cutting Meyer grew up in Guilford on her family farm in Guilford Center.

> *Me and my twin sister Marolyn loved to ice skate on the pond out in back of our house. We'd invite all the neighborhood girls over to enjoy the ice and we'd take turns shoveling it off. We were out back anytime we got the chance. Of course all of us kids had farming chores to do first, we fed the cows hay, cleaned out the gutters and my job was to strain the milk. We just went and had fun after that, and we'd skate until we got cold or it got dark. Mother would give us the devil if we came in late.*

Bill Vigneau also grew up in Brattleboro. He enjoyed skating on Vinton's Pond.

> *There was a paper mill where the Brattleboro Co-op is now. It was out behind the Billings Hotel before the Plaza was built. It wasn't all that big, but there was a place where we'd dam up the brook and it made a good place to skate.*
>
> *I knew Leslie W. Hill over at the Brattleboro Riding Club and Stables* [located at the corner of Orchard Street and Western Avenue]. *He owned one of the horses and he asked me one day, in 1943 around Christmastime, if I'd take a horse and go down and scrape off the ice for the people to skate. I was at the edge of the pond with the wooden scraper attached to the back of the horse when he broke right through the ice. I called my brother John up at the fire department and he came down with a few of the guys.*
>
> *To get the horse out of the water, we had to loop a rope around his neck and pull it like a noose to keep his head above the water. Each time he took a breath, we'd tighten the rope and then he floated to the top and the firemen rolled him out of the water.*
>
> *A woman who lived at 33 Canal Street saw us trying to get the horse out of the water and called the police because she thought we were beating up on the poor horse. But he got out okay, and I dried him off and walked him all the way back to West Brattleboro. He didn't so much as catch a cold.*

Brattleboro before Interstate 91

It was 1956. America was at war in Korea, the Cold War was in full swing and General Dwight D. Eisenhower was president of the United States. Many young men who had served as soldiers during World War II had taken advantage of the GI Bill, received a college education and had begun to settle into their private lives. Suburbia and the baby boomers were born. The national economy was rising for the first time in thirty years.

Most Americans owned an automobile and "motoring"—that is, driving vacations and Sunday afternoon jaunts in the car—were the norm. After the deprivations of life during the Second World War, folks were ready to relax, gasoline was cheap and it seemed that a road trip was the perfect way to enjoy a few hours of free time in the comfort of the Nash Rambler.

Farm equipment and automobiles shared the same roads, and unless there was a dotted yellow line on Route 5, there was no passing the hay wagon in front of you. But you could pass the time by singing "Heartbreak Hotel" on the radio along with Elvis Presley or discussing Grace Kelly marrying Prince Rainer III of Monaco while you waited to pass the tractor heading back to the farm.

Mom and pop cottages and motels dotted the roadways all over America. When a traveler ventured to Brattleboro, a room could be rented downstreet at the Brooks Hotel on the corner of Main and High Streets, at the Latchis Hotel or at the Billings Hotel, located where the Food Co-op now stands.

One could also venture just outside of town to Putney Road and rent a cottage at Snow White Cabins, located where McDonald's now stands, or at the new motor hotel called the Theatre Motor Lodge. If you rented a room on the back side, you could watch the drive-in movie on the big screen behind the motel while you stayed the night.

Dinner out could include the Royal Diner on Main Street or going up to Putney Road to King's Drive In, the Log Cabin Drive In or the Howard Johnson's Restaurant for its Friday all-you-could-eat fish fry. These restaurants were nestled into the areas around Geo. E. Thomas & Sons farms.

When entering Brattleboro from the south, cars wound through the countryside and farms dotting Route 5 through Guilford. All traffic went through downtown Brattleboro and emptied into two lanes that were Putney Road to the north. Around mid-afternoon, when local factories changed shifts, and again around 5:00 p.m. when businesses closed for the day, traffic crawled though Main Street simply because there was no other way to get home.

All that would change over the next five years in southern Vermont and across the nation. With heavy lobbying from the big three car manufacturers, planning for a federal highway system had begun in the 1930s, but it wasn't until 1956 that Congress funded the Dwight D. Eisenhower National System of Interstate and Defense Highways. The idea was to link the entire United

States, east to west and north to south, with a federally funded freeway. While Congress subsidized this new system of roads, they would be owned by the individual states in which they were built.

Eisenhower had experienced the German Autobahn network of roadways during World War II. He supported the idea of the national system of interstate highways to back the trucking industry, as a source of leisure for the American people and as an evacuation tool in the event of nuclear war or natural disaster. East–west routes for the interstate system were given even numbers and north–south routes were given odd numbers.

In Congress, senators began to lobby for the freeway to be built in their home states to support tourism and ease traffic troubles back home. The original plan called for the south–north interstate to be built through the state of New Hampshire, but due to the seniority of former governor and then U.S. senator George D. Aiken, Interstate 91 was routed through Vermont.

The process of buying the land for the freeway from local people began by 1957 as public meetings and engineers started to decide where the interstate highway would wind through the state.

Building Interstate 91

It could be said that Elva Brookes Pogar was an Interstate 91 bride. Pogar worked as a secretary for the Vermont State Highway District Office on Putney Road in Brattleboro. Her future husband, John Pogar, was a civil engineer who had been hired by the State of Vermont to decide where the new interstate highway would be located. They met and married in 1955.

"No aerial photographs were available to John until the project reached the Ascutney area, so he walked the land around the Massachusetts/Vermont border and had to decide where the road should go," remembers his wife. "One of his first assignments was to write a manual about what he was doing so that his work could be duplicated throughout the state. I knew shorthand, so we worked together in the evenings so that procedures could be published."

The State of Vermont was under pressure to get the project underway. Federal funding was available, but Vermont had begun its project later than other states. The survey crew worked quickly—and quietly. While Pogar chose the path of the interstate, other state employees hired to purchase the necessary land spoke directly with landowners about buying their property.

Opening day of Interstate 91, at exit two. *Left*: Erwin Powers in his Model T; *right*, Raymond S. Roberts in a brand-new car.

Robert Gaines, who together with his father owned the Gaines Farm in Guilford, was already familiar with state highways. The road in front of their farmhouse, Route 5, became a state highway in the early 1920s.

Gaines remembers,

> *The first indication of a new highway was when the surveyors came through our farm plodding out where they might put the road. They talked to my father and moved it east toward the mountain so that we wouldn't lose as much tillable land. The surveyor told my father that he thought the land to the east had too much ledge, but in the end, they moved the road to help us.*
>
> *They bought the land that is now the eastern side of the road because after the interstate was built, we no longer had access to it. We sold thirty of those acres at sixty dollars an acre. Vermont farmland didn't go for much. We didn't get too excited about it, not like people would today. Route 5 was getting congested. We were glad to have the interstate built to get the traffic out of our dooryard.*

As land was purchased toward Brattleboro, the state hit a snag. A local family who owned the property around exit one did not accept the dollar figure offered to them and took the state to court. Eminent domain was not yet a part of Vermont law. A price was eventually negotiated between the parties, but months passed in between, delaying construction.

As a consequence of the delay, those who represented the state in the purchase of land needed for the next leg of the project became less negotiable about the purchase price and more forceful in their tactics.

Shirley Sederquist Wright lived on Northern Avenue, a street that no longer exists in Brattleboro. Located between Brattle Street and Allerton Avenue, it housed approximately seven families. Dr. Grace Burnett's home and barns marked the beginning of Northern Avenue, turning off Western Avenue. Wright's grandmother purchased the family home around 1915. Her parents and sister lived in the upstairs apartment while her grandmother resided downstairs.

Wright recalls,

> *The state needed to purchase all the homes and land on Northern Avenue. They had just finished coming to an agreement with the family who took them to court and they were in no mood to negotiate about the price. They low balled us all.*
>
> *It was hard to find a new place to accommodate my grandmother and we had to move within a matter of a few months. Everybody on the street was bitter.*
>
> *The woods and meadows out behind Northern Avenue were beautiful. It was all land owned by the Retreat. We used to ski down the Retreat pastures. You can still see part of that hill on the northbound lane past exit two. Our living room is now in the middle of the southbound lane.*
>
> *In general it was felt that the interstate was a thing that should be done. It was to everyone's advantage and we knew that. At the time, however, I lost my home.*

Emma Bailey, America's First Female Auctioneer

"The Bailey Auction Barn on Black Mountain Road is prepared to handle auction sales. Courteous and efficient handling of all consignments, large or small. We will sell anything—from a plate to an estate, signed: Emma Bailey, Brattleboro's Woman Auctioneer."

This ad, placed in the *Brattleboro Reformer* in April 1950, created quite a stir in town. Emma P. Bailey, barely five feet tall, had decided to hold regular auctions at her barn on Black Mountain Road in Brattleboro. At the time, the majority of women were working at home caring for children and the household.

The Bailey family had purchased the former Bliss residence on Black Mountain Road in 1945. The place was such a wreck that three banks refused to give the Baileys a mortgage on the property, but Emma's husband, Jack, believed that he could do a great deal of the work himself and the Building and Loan Association supported their application for a mortgage.

Still, as Emma was fond of saying, "old houses are money hungry." And so it came to be that she proposed to her family that they take their love of attending country auctions to a new level—she suggested that she get her auctioneering license to supplement the family income.

Her daughter, Estelle Bailey Holmquist, remembers,

> *Mr. Sharon V. Holden and his wife, Grace, who owned Holden Antiques on Putney Road, became mentors for my mother. They taught her about the antique business.*
>
> *My father was a simple God-fearing man who did not like a lot of publicity, wanted to be able to provide for his wife and two daughters and worked hard at his job. But my mother knew she needed to help supplement the family income. My father didn't want her to work a daily job, but he supported her in becoming an auctioneer.*

Emma Bailey did some research and decided to apply to become a member of the National Auctioneering Association. Happy to see that the application did not specify whether she was male or female, she applied for a license. She was accepted into the association two years later in 1952, becoming the first female auctioneer in the United States.

She quickly ran into male prejudice. Her first auction was postponed for over a month when a local, rival auctioneer complained to the Town of Brattleboro that holding an auction at her home would be a violation of zoning regulations.

Emma recalled in an interview with the *Christian Science Monitor* in 1983,

> *I lost a very good auction one time because this male auctioneer and I both knew of a sale coming up. He went to the bank and said, "Well, I have a*

> *family to support, she only has a husband!" I didn't get the sale. This male auctioneer used sex in reverse to get that sale, and he used it many times. I never used it. I didn't want sex to be the tool. Men sell cars; women sell cars. There's no reason I can't sell antiques and understand them as well as a man.*

Bailey's auction became a local Saturday standard. Over the fifteen years she ran her business, her family was a big part of her team. Jack organized the goods to be sold, Emmy Lou did the record keeping of the sales and daughter Estelle ran a concession stand featuring tuna fish and egg salad sandwiches for twenty five cents, and soda for ten cents a cup.

Bailey wrote a book called *Sold to the Lady in the Green Hat* about her experiences. A popular hardback, it was reprinted three times, having been first published in 1962.

She gave up her business when her husband retired, but she went on to write columns for organic gardening magazines, a cookbook and an antique column for the *Vermonter Magazine*.

When asked why she retired at the height of her auction's popularity she answered, "It's like the old saying: leave a party while you still want to dance." Bailey died in 1999 at the age of eighty-nine.

Ray Pestle, County Agricultural Agent

Southern Vermont has traditionally been a place where agriculture thrives. Few have watched our rural heritage grow and change more than Ray Pestle. He held the position of county agricultural agent from 1945 to 1976, and continues to work with local farmers today even after retirement.

Ray commented,

> *I worked for the service in the golden age of County Extension. I've been very fortunate to have had a diverse background. I graduated from the University of Vermont in 1943 and from Rutgers Graduate School in 1945. My major at both schools was in dairy production, but through the years I gained a much more varied background in poultry, fruit orchards, vegetables and sugar making. Through my work at the County Extension I worked with a diverse audience and I enjoyed it.*

The census gave Windham County about six hundred full-time farms at the time I began my employment. When I came on the job, my co-worker Bruce Buchanan was a 4-H and County Club agent. He urged me to get out and meet them all. I met most of them. Not all of them were large producers, but it was a time when many people kept their own animals and grew vegetables.

I received a lot of calls and made visits to summer people. They owned quite a lot of the land here. They were a good asset to the town and the county. Some wanted to start their own gardens. Some wanted advice about what to do with some of their land, which had been farmed but was growing into goldenrod and brush. Often I was able to put them in touch with a nearby farmer to use the property as additional crop land, which was good for both parties.

Ray also helped neighbors make agreements for longer-term use of our county's agricultural land.

Around 1947, I met with George Ranney who owned the land that is now called Sweet Tree Farm, and Fred Vanderwater, who owned the adjoining land. We put together an agreement in writing, which provided for the use of fields, which would be limed, fertilized and reseeded. No money was exchanged and the agreement became a working operation. If either party died, the agreement could be extended to Mr. Ranney's son and to Mr. Vanderwater's wife. And in fact, that is just what happened. Even though the farm was sold, the agreement has survived. I believe it is a great accomplishment to have such an arrangement take place for the good of the parties involved and the use of the land.

Most of Ray's work was as an agricultural practitioner.

I worked with vegetable and small fruit farmers, and answered many questions every day ranging from insect problems on a plant or vegetable to helping someone with a strawberry that was malformed, to answering questions that came in the mail. We made reports to the University of Vermont, and handled more office calls and telephone calls than any other county in the state. It was a busy office and very interesting work.

Federal, state and county taxes paid for salary and mileage. The County Extension office was rounded out with the knowledge of County Forester

Gil Cameron and Halsey Hicks. Ruth Hertzberg was also on the team to handle questions concerning food, nutrition and clothing.

> *The local agricultural community could also join the Farm Bureau for a membership fee of five or six dollars a year. The first president of the Farm Bureau was a man by the name of George Aiken.* [Mr. Aiken went on to become governor and a U.S. senator from Vermont for many years.] *Headquarters for the Farm Bureau and the County Extension were in the same office. I had the privilege of working with some very fine people. Anyone could be a member, businesses on Main Street joined too. It was a different era.*

Though retired, Ray is still working. "People still call me occasionally. I do some private consulting work for larger farms on plant health problems, weeds and insects, that sort of thing. With the spotlight on organic farming, I've received more calls. I don't go out looking for work, but when people call, I'm always glad to help them."

Bruce Corwin, Leader of the Band

According to his mother, Bruce Corwin sat in front of the radio as a small child and tried to direct the music. He began taking piano lessons at the age of four, and by fourth grade Frank Bush, the music teacher in Bellows Falls, handed him a trombone. It was love at first slide.

"I just loved the feel of that instrument and had learned to play a scale by supper time," laughed Corwin. Bruce graduated from Bellows Falls High School in 1951 and, not feeling at first that music should be his career, went to Orono, Maine, to study forestry.

"I wanted to get out there and talk with the trees, but by the second year, I decided that the trees could talk to themselves," Corwin chuckles, "I switched majors and graduated with a bachelor of arts in music. I've been playing an instrument ever since. In college I took a class where I had to learn to play every instrument in the band. I can still do that, but not, of course, very well."

He started his career in Bennington. Corwin remembers,

> *By then I was married and raising a family, and so even though my preference would have been to teach instrumental music, I taught choral*

> *music instead for a few years, then I switched back and taught instrumental music in Brattleboro.*
>
> *In 1967 I received a fellowship from the National Defense Education Act, and moved the family over to Durham, New Hampshire, so that I could get a master's degree. I always knew that to teach most effectively, you need to get inside the eyes of a kid, so my master's degree is in counseling. I was all set to take a counseling job in Brattleboro in 1969 but the budget was cut and so I continued on with teaching music.*

In 1972, Corwin went to teach in Townsend and, after a number of years there, returned to the smaller towns outside of Brattleboro. He retired in 1993 after a thirty-eight-year career in the field.

Even though his days were always filled with music, Corwin has also managed to be a member of several bands. He's been a part of the Grafton Cornet Band since 1944, and has been its director for over twenty years as well.

"Music keeps me young," says Corwin. "A musician plays the instrument, and the director plays the whole band. I tell the bands I direct, there may be forty of you, but there's only one of me, so we better be listening to each other. We have an awful lot of fun together."

Corwin was also a member of the Chester Brass Band. Its eight to twelve members got together about once a week to play. In the late 1980s, members of the 172nd Infantry band at the American Legion contacted Chester Brass.

> *There were a bunch of the guys still getting together to play, Bill and Joe Holiday, Harvey Dix, Merrill Harris, Bert Martin, Maynard Walker among them. They wanted to know if some of us could join them so that they could continue to play. We were happy to do it. One evening, we were playing at the Legion and Don Long asked me if I was willing to direct the American Legion Band and find some more members. We created a committee, put out the word and about twenty people came to the first rehearsal. We've been going strong for sixteen years since.*

The Brattleboro American Legion Band went to Salt Lake City, Utah, in August 2006, where members earned second place in a national competition of Legion bands.

We went to a competition in Charlotte, North Carolina, not too long ago. We came in at fourth place and we beat out a band from Kansas City that had been there forever. We're excited to be going to Salt Lake. We're not only the Brattleboro American Legion Band; we're the only Legion band in the state of Vermont. Governor Douglas calls us the Vermont State Legion Band. We've played in the legislative chamber, we've led the parade at the Big E on Vermont day and we've played in Montpelier for World War II veterans who've finally been able to collect their medals. It's been quite a ride.

Fire Chief David Emery

Fire Chief David Emery keeps a hectic schedule. Within a week's time, the Wilder Building burned, but his department's obligations do not end when the fire is out. Chief Emery had meetings scheduled all week with town officials, insurance representatives and engineers. These duties transpired in addition to his customary responsibilities as fire chief.

He doesn't mind. "I look forward to coming to work, every single day. I still get that feeling when I come in the door every morning like when we are little kids and we visit the firehouse for the first time, and you know what? We still do the same thing we've always done here, we just do it better."

Chances are his first time in the door was at a tender age. David grew up in Vernon and comes from a family of firefighters. Tradition continues as his two sons join him at the firehouse.

David started his career as chief of the Brattleboro Fire Department—for one day. He chuckles as he tells the story.

In 1970, the Elks Club arranged for the local high school students to job shadow adults in the community. I worked with Fire Chief T. Howard Mattison for the day. We were called to a car fire and I rode in the back of the fire engine with my eyes as big as can be, and when I hopped off the truck, one of the guys looked me in the eye and said, "Okay, Chief, what do you want." I learned right then how much I didn't know and how much there was to learn. After my first big day as chief I got busted back down to the bottom of the ladder and had to work my way back up.

Woolworth and W.T. Grant stores, where Key Bank and Candle in the Night are now located.

David graduated from Brattleboro Union High School, filled in as a temporary firefighter over the summer and then went on to become a full-time member of the department. During those years, he also spent time training in Boston when the city was alive with racial tension due to forced busing, and fires were an everyday, sometimes every hour, occurrence. "I learned a lot down there," he said, as he told stories of a city under siege.

On November 20, 1972, David and two other firefighters found themselves in dangerous circumstances in the basement of the Woolworth fire on Main Street, where Candle in the Night is currently located.

> *Firefighting was a much different deal back then. We were well trained and as well equipped as anybody at that time, but we were essentially dressed in cotton coats and jeans with helmets that didn't protect much of our heads or necks. We were all just plain lucky that day.*
>
> *Essentially, the same scenario played out with the Wilder Building fire. The difference was, Chris and Greg* [the two firefighters who were almost trapped during a flash over] *were on the fourth floor and I had been in the basement, and we had multiple good things going for us. We had great training and experience, and we have equipment that is top shelf.*

The Wilder fire consumed two sets of coats and pants at $2,982, two helmets at $1,000 and two air packs at $4,400 that need replacement. Insurance will cover some of the price tag; the rest will have to come out of the budget. It's a hefty expense, but this gear saved the lives of two men. If it had not been top-shelf equipment, the story might have had a different ending. The taxpayers have always been understanding and supportive about the needs of our department and we've always been appreciative of that.

We have a dedicated firefighting team in Brattleboro and all the departments in the surrounding areas work well together. Every single Brattleboro firefighter showed up for the Wilder Building fire. That's an unusual thing. It is the guys in this department who make the difference because every single one of them is here because they want to be. They may have different motivations, but they all want to be here and be part of this team. That creates an amazing atmosphere. I've been here for thirty-four years, and you know what? If I had it to do all over again, I wouldn't change a thing.

1960s postcard.

THE 1960s AND 1970s

How a Ski Resort Changed an Entire Town

Each Sunday, Cedar Street is filled with vehicles from "away," clearly tourists, skiers in particular, driving back to their homes having spent the weekend in Vermont.

This phenomenon is still new to our state. The last of the "big three" ski areas was Stratton Mountain, which opened in 1962 to great fanfare and little reservation. Then Governor Keyser came to ski with his young son, Chris, on opening day. Men dressed in suits and the then fashionable thin neckties gave speeches in the new alpine-themed hall. Skiers laced up their leather ski boots, strapped on their wooden skis with thin metal cables and hit the new slopes, while one hundred or so people dressed in fur coats or ski sweaters listened to the speeches of the day. Big business had come to southern Vermont.

A special edition of the *Brattleboro Reformer* dated January 30, 1962, marked the opening of the mountain.

> *From the summer of 1960 to the winter of 1962 is a short span of time in which to transform the face of a mountain into a major ski area. Yet 12 trails, a 4 story Tyrolean base lodge, 3 double chair lifts, an alpine village and a network of roads now exist on Stratton Mountain where there were only thousands of acres of forest 2 years ago…*
>
> *The Stratton Ski Area has been alive with activity since it started its chairlifts for the Christmas holidays. It already has enjoyed some excellent skiing conditions, but also has proved its trails are skiable even when abnormal conditions have shut down other areas…*

September 23, 1960, in a clearing and construction operation, affecting more than 1,000 acres, Vermont contractors are turning this mountain wilderness into a major ski and recreations area. During the past few months, the Stratton developers have been engaged in a giant clearing, cutting, filling and grading operations to complete a 2-mile road…

Big business is coming to Stratton and Winhall too, but the less than 300 persons who make up the two small towns are viewing the future "boom" with reserved optimism.

Principals in the huge endeavor staged an outdoor barbecue among cinder blocks and crude foundation beginnings of the mammoth lodge [two years prior, at the beginning of construction]. *Some 50 persons, including officers of the two towns and their families, munched chicken at the construction site—and talked the future.*

But it is with a provisional sort of reserved optimism that many people among Stratton's 270 odd population are looking forward to the "new industry."

The attitude is much the same among Winhall's 245 citizens.

"We think it's good. Most people do," said a Stratton housewife surveying the muddy area where selectmen of the two towns were chatting with the developers.

"Not everyone is so sure," she added, "but time will tell."

Stratton Selectman Ralph Pike observed that "land values are bound to go up around here—they already have; some, anyway."

Affecting an estimated 1,000 acres, the major development, which will be graded to a year round recreational center, hopes to have three double chair lifts totaling 9,500 feet in length ready for hickory lovers at the beginning of the winter of 1961–1962.

The shell of the 100 by 150 feet three-story base lodge is expected to be completed by December 28 of this year. It will be located on the northeast slope below lift lines with a view across the West River Valley to Bromley.

From the summit of Stratton Mountain, Mt. Snow will loom in clear view to the south.

And this is perhaps the key, developers say, to the site choice which rests in one of the East's heaviest snow belts: Stratton Mountain will complete a three barreled ski development chain—Mt Snow, Stratton and Bromley.

"It will probably bring more business around here—lodging places, eating facilities and employment for some of the men," said a quiet man standing apart from the barbecue crowd.

"We see a bright future," said a woman seated at an improvised barbecue table, "but there is some question of what kind of people will be coming in—the recreation trade, I mean."

Patrolling the Slopes

When Brattleboro resident Ruth Lane began downhill skiing, there were a number of ski areas nearby, almost all of which have since closed. Opening in the mid-1940s, Pinetop Ski Area was located in Vernon. It had three rope tows, a vertical drop of four hundred feet and four trails. Pinetop also had great flood lighting and was a popular area for night skiing. It featured the area's only Tiny Tot Tow, where kids as young as three and a half could learn to ski. Pinetop closed in the mid-'60s.

Lane's brother-in-law, Arnold Lane, persuaded her and her husband Eugene to join the ski patrol in 1956. "I had only been on skis for one year," recalled Ruth recently. "However, we enrolled in first aid courses, and also took classes in avalanche and mountaineering rescue, which was taught by Nick Collins, now a sixty-year member of the Brattleboro Ski Patrol."

That year was the beginning of a forty-one-year membership with the ski patrol for Lane, a legacy that earned her an award in 1982 as a National Appointee Outstanding Member. Lane remarked,

> *The Brattleboro Ski Patrol was founded in 1938 by Bruce Buchanan with five patrolmen. Woodstock had the first rope tow in the state. By the time I was involved there was a second rope tow on Guilford Street where the current Memorial Park is now located, and then it was moved to Bonnyvale Road, and then to the Latchis Ski Jump area out behind where Rescue Inc. is now located on the other side of the interstate.* [Before it was built] *I also patrolled the Harris Hill Ski Jump, Memorial Park, Maple Valley and on Hogback Mountain.*
>
> *The Brattleboro Ski Patrol didn't join as members of the National Ski Patrol until 1941. There were nine charter members, including Francis "Ozzie" Stowell, who still lives locally. Medical advisors also considered honorary members included Dr. Philip H. Wheeler and Dr. James Miniszek.*
>
> *During the 1962–63 seasons, the Brattleboro Ski Patrol was awarded nationally as being one of the five best outfits in the nation. By that*

time there were around seventy-five members in our local chapter. Walter Harrington was in charge. He had high expectations of us all and we all respected him. He was very proud of our patrol.

A roster was made each week letting every member know who was going to be at which ski area. There was paid staff during the week, and the volunteers worked the weekends. Six to eight members would work each ski area, with two professional ski patrol members to oversee the volunteers.

Each member skied with a first aid belt. There was a sled loaded on top of the mountain that contained splints, traction irons and cravats. If the sled was needed, a patroller would ski the sled down to the accident and onto the base of the mountain, where a tractor would transport the injured from the base to the first aid room. Later on, walkie-talkies were issued to members to save that step in an emergency.

"Of course, you never knew what type of accident you would encounter," says Lane. "We'd always have the usual cuts and bruises and the occasional broken limb. Those were the days before we had rescue squads, but we had a van that transported out to the hospital."

Lane started out on Northland Wooden Skis, cable bindings, lace-up boots made of leather and wooden poles with wide leather baskets in the center, but for the last thirty-five years, she's been skiing on Rossignols.

There have been a lot of changes in the industry over the years. Equipment has changed, areas were able to begin making man-made snow, and communication equipment has improved. But the basics of the ski patrol have not shifted. It's still a great opportunity to serve the public, to help out where you can.

I gave up my membership in 1997, but I'm still out skiing with my grown children and my grandkids. Ski patrol was a great way to make it affordable to ski as a family. All our kids learned how to ski and we were all out on the slopes at least every weekend.

ORIGINS OF RESCUE

"Several years ago when we were holding a squad meeting, a man whose life we had saved appeared during the meeting with tears streaming down his face. He walked through the room thanking each member of the Rescue

Inc. squad. Those are the moments that stick with me," said Verne Bristol, one of the founding members of Rescue Inc.

In the early 1960s, a group of fifteen local men who were National Ski Patrol members and volunteer firemen began to talk about starting up a rescue squad. It was before the interstate came through town and accidents were a common phenomenon at places with names like Richardson Dip, Chicken Coop Hill and Dead Man's Gulch.

Bristol remembered,

> *All those places on the secondary roads have been fixed, but fifty years ago, it was in those places that accidents happened repeatedly. When the telephone rang to call us to the scene of an accident, we didn't need to hear that it was located five miles south on Route 5, all we needed to hear was that there was another accident at Ryan's Curve in Guilford.*

These volunteers had no building, no radios, no supplies and no money, but were filled with a desire to serve their community.

"The budget for the organization is now well over $2.5 million, but when we started, we had $10. A local car dealership sold us an old station wagon for $1. Half the time it wouldn't even start in the winter. Three of us would get out and push it to get it going," said Bristol.

Dr. James Miniszek was Rescue Inc.'s first medical director. Maude Rounds, who owned an answering service, volunteered to call when there was a need to round up the members. Bristol recalled,

> *We called them our "call girls." Maude would call me, I'd leave for the call and my wife would call two more members, their wives would make two more calls until we all received the word.*
>
> *Finally, as time went by we received an anonymous donation of $2,000 with which we purchased a white van. But in those days we still didn't transport any patients. The local funeral homes dispatched a hearse and a member rode in back with the patient. I could tell you stories about some of those drivers. They weren't trained to drive hurt people, they were trained to drive dead ones.*

With the support of local people, eventually an abandoned gas station on Canal Street was bought and renovated to serve as Rescue Inc.'s first home.

Until then we parked the van out behind Pliny Park. When it snowed and the town had plowed the roads, we'd drive to the truck only to find it socked in with five feet of snow. Sometimes the truck wouldn't start and we'd have to jump it. If we were able to get to a call in thirty minutes in those days, that was a good response time.

We always had the support of the local people. Early on, I asked for donations to support our organization and received $105,000 in $5 and $10 bills. That was quite a thing. If one or two people each gave $50,000 that would have been different, but when you receive support from ten thousand people in small amounts, that lets you know there is grass-roots support for what you're doing.

Bristol eventually became CEO of an organization that ran seventeen calls in its first year and almost several thousand calls the year he retired in 1997.

We were the first squad in the state to do IVs in the field. We always had a great relationship with Brattleboro Memorial Hospital and relied on them for on-going training. Over the years we've earned all manner of awards, from the State Department of Motor Vehicles, from the Vermont State Police and recognized as the best rescue squad in the state of Vermont. We've always been ahead of the pack.

But of all the things we've done, I'm most proud of the men and women who have served Rescue Inc. over the years. There are many more of them out there than people realize. I still miss working with Rescue Inc. These are fine people who give up so much of their time to continue the training that allows them the honor of serving their community.

THE POWER OF ONE VOTE

Second Circuit Court of Appeals senior judge James L. Oakes has been a Vermonter for fifty-nine years. A Harvard Law School graduate, he initially made his way to Vermont in 1947 and opened a law practice with state senator Robert T. Gannett.

Charles Ross, who was public service commissioner under Governor Robert Stafford, contacted Oakes in the late 1950s. Oakes and Ross joined forces and represented the public before the Public Service Commission.

The Honorable James L. Oakes. *Courtesy of Jason Henske.*

Their jobs were varied and included negotiating a long-term power authority contract with the State of New York.

Then U.S. senator George D. Aiken had been instrumental in passing a federal bill involving St. Lawrence Power in the state of New York. The new law gave neighboring states up to 10 percent of the power produced from hydropower on the St. Lawrence River. Ross and Oakes negotiated the terms of the contract.

Meanwhile Oakes, a Republican, ran for and was elected to the state legislature. He then ran for a second term unopposed. Oakes thought his popularity with both Democrats and Republicans was enough to run for lieutenant governor in 1964, but he was defeated by Richard Snelling in the election.

Two years passed without Oakes in the legislature. In the meantime, in 1965, the House was reapportioned from 246 members, representing each town in the state, to 150 seats, with districts based on population. Before the reapportionment, Republicans had dominated the legislature. The reapportionment added a significant enough number of Democrats that they carried the majority of the new, smaller House.

In 1965, Fredrick J. Fayette, secretary of the Democratic Party, had introduced a bill that had Governor Phil Hoff's backing. It was a bill to create a power authority in Vermont patterned on those in Oregon and Washington States, somewhat like the current contract with New York State.

This bill was going to enable Vermont to buy power from Hydro-Quebec. Having built many new dams in the 1960s, Hydro-Quebec had power in abundance and was anxious to sell the extra for a good and low price.

Central Vermont Public Service, Green Mountain Power and Citizen's Utilities opposed this bill. They were the three biggest sellers of power in Vermont, and all favored nuclear energy. Their argument was that they could produce power that would be less expensive than Hydro-Quebec.

Oakes and others who favored Hydro-Quebec had retained an expert from the Public Service Commission in New York who was familiar with the workings of atomic plants. All were concerned with the ideas that nuclear plants eventually wear out, that the environment would be adversely affected and that the cost of a nuclear plant had to be absorbed within thirty to thirty-five years to be considered profitable.

Oakes felt that there was no way that those who favored nuclear energy in Vermont could live up to the promises being made to the legislature.

Cooperatives and municipal utilities in Vermont engaged Oakes to lobby in the legislature in order to promote the Fayette Bill, which favored Hydro-Quebec. He felt that his work would improve with the help of Franklin S. Billings Jr., who had been Speaker of the House, to assist him in this work. The two men divided up their tasks. Oakes would lobby the Senate and Billings would lobby the House with assistance from Oakes.

When the Fayette Bill was introduced in the Senate, there was no problem in achieving Senate passage of the bill. A healthy majority easily won the vote.

But both Billings and Oakes knew that there would be a tighter vote in the House. They began to track the records of each House member, hoping to pass the Hydro-Quebec Bill and defeat those who wanted the nuclear energy bill to pass. They believed they could count on the majority, which was Democratic, because fellow Democrat Governor Hoff also supported the Hydro-Quebec Bill.

Oakes was living in Guilford. The town of Guilford had been reapportioned to be part of the same legislative district as Vernon. Oakes soon saw that he wasn't going to make much headway with the Guilford representative. Vernon was part of his district, and the town was the proposed site of a nuclear power plant that was strongly supported by residents. Guilford had a more neutral stance toward nuclear energy.

Very soon, Billings and Oakes wrote off lobbying the representative from Guilford. But one day, in the House, Oakes was amazed to see the Guilford representative speak with a Democratic representative, a woman, from the Barre area.

He wondered what he would be interested in saying to her and he soon discovered that the Guilford representative was trying to persuade her to vote for the nuclear plant and against the power authority bill.

The day before the bill was to be voted, Oakes spoke with the woman from Barre and gave her a final pitch. She still seemed doubtful.

"The vote was by alphabet or area, but whatever it was, she came up the wrong way and the bill failed by one vote. That meant that the atomic plant would be built and Hydro-Quebec power went down the tubes," remembered Oakes recently.

The legislature officially adjourned, and as was custom at the time, many representatives met for a legislative party at a tavern across from the statehouse. At the end of the evening, as Oakes was walking toward the statehouse to pick up his belongings, he noticed the representative from Guilford and the representative from Barre walking hand in hand across the parking lot.

Oakes said,

> *Within practically no time, both those representatives left their families and the state and took off to Las Vegas, where they divorced and were remarried to one another.*
>
> *I remember being contacted by a newspaperman who was going to reveal all of this in a news story. Out of friendship to the family, I told him that he shouldn't do that and as far as I know it was never publicized. This was unique in my legislative experience and it was terribly important to the history of the state. We all shook our heads for a long time after that.*

Oakes went on to become the attorney general of Vermont from 1967 to 1969, was appointed U.S. district judge in 1970 and then, in 1971, to the United States Court of Appeals, where he has continued to serve as judge for the past thirty-five years.

Brattleboro postcard, 1912.